Prentice-Hall, Inc., Englewood Cliffs, N.J.

Work in
Traditional
and
Modern
Society

STANLEY H. UDY, JR. Yale University

Current printing (last digit):
10 9 8 7 6 5 4 3 2 1

P-13-967554-X
C-13-967562-O

Library of Congress Catalog Card Number: 73-99741

Printed in the United States of America

FOR LEE, MARTHA, AND ELIZABETH

PRENTICE-HALL INTERNATIONAL, INC.
London

PRENTICE-HALL OF AUSTRALIA, PTY. LTD.
Sydney

PRENTICE-HALL OF CANADA, LTD.
Toronto

PRENTICE-HALL OF INDIA PRIVATE LTD.
New Delhi

PRENTICE-HALL OF JAPAN, INC.
Tokyo

WILBERT E. MOORE / NEIL J. SMELSER   Editors

Modernization of Traditional Societies Series

The twentieth century will be called many things by future historians—the Age of Global War, perhaps, the Age of Mass Society, the Age of the Psychoanalytic Revolution, to name a few possibilities. One name that historians certainly will not fail to give our century is the Age of the New Nation. For, evidently, the convulsive emergence of the colonies into independence and their subsequent struggle to join the ranks of the prosperous, powerful, and peaceful is the most remarkable revolution of our time. Taking the world as a whole, men are now preoccupied with no subject more than they are with the travail of the New Nations.

The world of the social sciences has been studying the pace of social change in these newly emergent areas, and from time to time has been engaging in technical assistance and even in the giving of advice on high levels of social strategy. Little of this effort has reached publicly accessible form. Though technical treatises abound, and isolated, journalistic reports of distinctly exotic countries are not wanting, college curricula have scarcely reflected either the scientific endeavors or the world-wide revolutions in technology and in political affairs.

This series on "Modernization of Traditional Societies" is designed to inform scholars, students, and citizens about the way quiet places have come alive, and to introduce at long last materials on the contemporary character of

EDITORIAL FOREWORD

developing areas into college curricula for the thought leaders of the near future. To these ends we have assembled experts over the range of the social sciences and over the range of the areas of the underdeveloped and newly developing sections of the earth that were once troublesome only to themselves.

We are proud to be participants in this series, and proud to offer each of its volumes to the literate world, with the hope that that world may increase, prosper, think, and decide wisely.

WILBERT E. MOORE

NEIL J. SMELSER

Contents

Tables

Figures

The organization of work and the process of social and economic development are topics that have interested sociologists for a long time. Each of these areas has, in its own right, given rise to a very extensive literature, yet by and large these two topics have seldom been explored in relation to one another. Most studies of organized work have been restricted to modern industrial society, and very few analyses of social and economic development have focussed specifically on the role of work organization in such development. This little book represents an attempt to bring these two fields closer together and, in the process, to provide more information about both of them. Specifically, we propose to investigate the part played by work organization in the transition from traditional to modern industrial society. The modernization process has been studied frequently and from a variety of points of view, but the possibility that the way in which work is organized in traditional society may have some effect on modernization has almost never been suggested. It is precisely that possibility which we propose to investigate. As a by-product of this investigation, we will explore in a more general way the implications of the relationship between social development and organized work for organization theory. We shall pursue these interests by exploring two rather simple working hypotheses. The first is that prevailing forms of work organization in any society affect the po-

CHAPTER ONE   tential of that society for social and economic

Organized Work and Social Development

development. The second asserts that the state of development of any society affects the way in which work is likely to be organized in that society. Essentially this entire book is an elaboration of these two hypotheses as they apply to the modernization of traditional society.

Our first task will be to set forth precisely what we mean by both "organized work" and "social development," and to propose some general hypotheses about their interrelations. This is the subject matter of Chapter One. Using this discussion as a point of departure, and with the aid of cross-cultural comparative data, Chapter Two then analyses the state of work organization in traditional society, in light of preindustrial patterns of social development. Chapter Three treats the part played by work organization in the transition from traditional to modern industrial society. Finally, Chapters Four and Five discuss the resultant organizational characteristics and problems of modern industrial work.

We should perhaps also make clear what this book is *not* about. In particular, it is not about industrial and economic development generally, but only about the role of organized work in such development. Many topics familiar to the student of general economic and industrial development thus emerge here as "external conditions" relative to work organization, rather than as objects of study in their own right. We shall, for example, not be interested in exploring such problems as how and why a commercialized market economy develops, or even how industrial technology per se, as a system of knowledge and capabilities, comes into being. Rather, we shall be interested only in how and at what points such contextual conditions interact with work organization, and with what consequences. By the same token, this book is not about general organization theory, but about the implications of social development for organized work. Our treatment of organization is limited to spelling out such implications, and thus does not include many other important aspects of administration that might be of interest to the student of organizations generally. In short, although we seek here to deal with both organized work and social development, we shall deal with each of these topics only insofar as it relates to the other.

THE NATURE OF ORGANIZED WORK

What is work and what happens when it is organized? Most people think of work as some activity that entails physical and mental effort. Beyond this point of agreement one encounters a wide variety of notably contradictory ideas about what work is. Economists, in effect, define work as something that is useful. Most people agree that at least some work is essential. Some people believe that work is morally good, yet work is also something that we probably wouldn't do quite so much of if we didn't have to. Both the Puritan ethic and modern organizational psychology are often rather frenetic in insisting that work is something of an ennobling venture in which man should find self-fulfillment. At the same time, the Judaeo-Christian religious tradition portrays work as a perpetual punishment suffered by mankind as a result of some primordial catastrophe. Work, whatever it is, is certainly something about which people seem to be extraordinarily ambivalent. Furthermore, this ambivalence is by no means confined to modern Western culture. Ideas to the effect that work is so good that some of it should always be left for tomorrow are found almost everywhere.[1]

"Work" Defined

Why this seeming ambivalence? The central problem is that work, to a greater extent than other activities, is both physical and social at the same time. In order both to capture, and yet be able to explore, this dual character, we shall define *work* very simply as any purposive human effort to modify man's physical environment. This definition is intentionally minimal and narrow, precisely because we wish to explore its implications, and to do so across a variety of cultures. Therefore, beyond prescribing that work must be purposive, we do not include any psychological requirements, for example that work be something people feel obliged to do whether they want to or not. Whether people consider their work useful, difficult, pleasant, profitable, and so forth, are questions we shall explore empirically under varying conditions. Also, because we shall wish to examine work in a variety of primitive, traditional, and modern cultural settings, we have eschewed culture-bound economic considerations from our definition: for example, that work must be an activity engaged in by people to earn a livelihood in a market economy. Again, in certain of the cultural contexts we shall examine, the question of the extent to which work in fact enters into the market system is itself important, and must be faced empirically. Similarly, the possibility of defining work simply as an activity considered utilitarian was rejected, because such a definition proved very difficult to apply operationally in cross-cultural research.

Our definition has the further advantage of permitting us to treat various work-connected activities such as administration, management, public relations, politics, research, and so forth, as being conceptually distinct from work itself. We can, for example, raise questions about how

[1] For a general discussion of the philosophy and ideology of work see Adriano Tilgher, *Work: What It Has Meant to Men through the Ages*, trans. D. C. Fisher (London: George G. Harrap, 1931).

much administration is present relative to the amount of work performed under various cultural and technological conditions. However unacceptable the conception of administration as "overhead" might be to the economist interested in aggregate activity levels in a modern economy, this conception is far from useless to the organization theorist or to the manager facing alternative ways of designing administrative structures. Thus, by our definition, administrators, managers, researchers, and lawyers, though they may toil mightily, do not "work" (unless it can be shown in any given case that their efforts are directed toward modification of the physical environment). Rather, they administer, manage, do research, and practice law. All of these activities, certainly, are exceedingly important, particularly in certain cultures. However, we wish to be able to consider them as related to work in different ways under different conditions, rather than as part of a cultural universal we call "work."

At the same time, our definition of work is perhaps less narrow than it might at first appear. The concept of "modifying the physical environment" can be very broadly construed. It includes not only the production of material goods, but also such activities as transportation and other services that leave the environment in some changed physical state. Thus our definition of work describes an activity that is culturally universal, and at the same time says no more about it than is absolutely essential. We can thus raise the question empirically as to whether work, under given conditions, does or does not tend to possess other attributes.

Let us now return to our earlier statement that work is both markedly physical and markedly social at the same time. This characteristic of work is important because physical and social forces are ultimately independent of one another in origin. The combination of physical and social constraints to which work is subject is therefore always to some extent and in some ways inconsistent.[2] It is thus neither a chance occurrence nor a vagary of some particular culture that people should feel ambivalent about work. Probably in no other area of human life are the intrinsic strains between the physical and social worlds felt so directly and immediately, and we have all felt them. Simply because the tool and die maker takes pride in his craft does not mean that he might not frequently rather be at home with his family, and the executive who

[2] See Georges Friedmann, Pierre Naville, *et al.*, *Traité de sociologie du travail* (Paris: Librarie Armand Colin, 1961), I, 11-34.

complains about long hours may well at the same time be very enthusiastic about his job.

Organized Work and Its Constraints: a Model

These strains are particularly evident in *organized* work; that is, work carried on by several persons acting in concert, rather than by one person alone. Organization complicates the work situation, not only by increasing the number of ways in which strain can be felt, but by multiplying the number of ways of coping with it. We shall thus think of all organized work as carried on in the context of a *work system;* that is, a work organization pursuing production objectives by means of a technology. A *work organization* is a group of people behaving in accordance with a system of roles expressly designed for the purpose of performing work; and *technology* is the totality of combinations of activities and facilities through which production objectives, broadly or narrowly conceived, can be achieved. All work systems exist in the context of a broader *social setting* and are, further, subject to *physical exigencies* in their internal relationships.

Social constraints. The principal pattern of constraints generated by this combination of social influences and physical exigencies is shown in Figure 1.1. In the first place, the content and form of each component

FIGURE 1.1

The Work System and Its Constraints

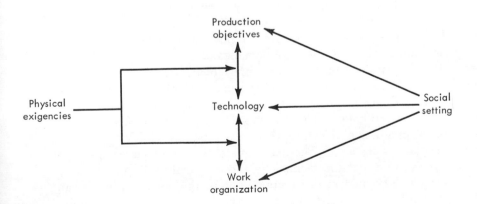

of the work system is limited by purely social possibilities. No given production objective will be pursued, or even necessarily thought of, unless it is a meaningful and culturally valued end in the social setting. Similarly, no technology and no organizational form can be exploited unless it is, or can be made to be, culturally meaningful and socially acceptable. Obvious extreme examples readily come to mind: few buggy whips are made today, airplanes did not exist in ancient Greece, and the indigenous Australian aborigines did not possess limited liability corporations.

Physical constraints. Turning now to the opposite side of Figure 1.1, the range of possible relationships between the components of the work system is at the same time limited by purely physical exigencies. For purely physical reasons, no given set of production objectives can be achieved through just any technology, and no given technology can be carried on by just any work organization. It is clear, to give some obvious examples, that automobiles cannot be produced by the same technology as is used to grow corn, and that no technology physically suited to the mass production of automobiles can—barring some as yet hypothetical form of sophisticated automation—be carried on by a work organization consisting of only five persons. Similarly, no given work organization can carry on just any technology and no given technology can be employed to achieve just any set of production objectives. If work is to take place, production objectives, technology, and work organization structure must be physically adapted to one another. Any given state of any one of these three components immediately places purely physical limits on the possible forms the other two can assume.

Incompatibilities. All of this seems evident enough. Organized work cannot be carried on unless it is socially acceptable, and it cannot be performed unless it is physically possible. The problem is that it is impossible for all aspects of work to meet physical exigencies and at the same time uniformly conform to all demands of social acceptability. Any technology physically suited to the achievement of a given set of production objectives will always involve some activities that are simply not culturally defined, and it is also very likely to entail some activities that are considered undesirable or even socially prohibited. The fact that some set of production objectives themselves may be highly valued and very acceptable does not, furthermore, guarantee the social acceptability of all—or even any—of the technology those objectives imply. Automobiles are highly valued in our culture, but in the course of producing them assembly line workers engage in many activities that are highly monotonous, repetitive, and fractionated, and, if we are to believe research results, conducive to actual social alienation.[3] Furthermore, research on "informal organization" in industry has long found a variety of *ad hoc* activities—some of which are likely to become patterned in the course of time—to be essential to the success of virtually any kind of industrial production, and has shown that some of the most important ones are precisely those that do run counter to cultural norms.[4] Control tower personnel in New York airports, for example, claim that they often face the choice of observing the rules or bringing the planes in on time. In a more extreme way, it is by no means uncommon to find highly valued production objectives for which no known physically adequate technology even exists. No cure for cancer has yet been developed, for example. However, the case of the valued objective with no known technology is an extreme one.

The main point is that the successful physical adaptation of any technology to any production objective always involves some activities that in varying degrees run counter to social demands. It is thus impossible for any such adaptation to be made while, at the same time, both production objectives and technology remain equally constrained by the social setting, as shown in Figure 1.1.

The same argument can be made with respect to the achievement of socially acceptable production objectives by any given socially acceptable technology. As a minimum, every technology generates certain by-products that run counter to social norms, in the course of producing something otherwise quite acceptable. Automobiles are not supposed to produce air pollution, but they do. Again, there are more extreme possibilities. Medical technology could be used for the purpose of killing rather than curing; and some firms go out of business because they cannot produce anything that enough people want to buy. The main point, again, is that every technology entails some physical consequences of at least problematical social acceptability. For this reason, production objectives and technology cannot both be physically adapted to each other and socially adapted to the setting at the same time.

It is similarly the case that technology and work organization structure cannot be mutually adapted physically, while still remaining equally socially constrained. If technology is taken as "given," the organizational work positions it implies are always, in some respects and to some degree,

[3] Robert Blauner, *Alienation and Freedom* (Chicago: Chicago University Press, 1964); Charles R. Walker and Robert H. Guest, *The Man on the Assembly Line* (New Haven: Yale University Press, 1952).

[4] See for example Alvin W. Gouldner, *Patterns of Industrial Bureaucracy* (New York: The Free Press, 1954).

of dubious general social reference. This problem is, as a matter of fact, particularly acute in modern industrial society, where the central position of occupation in the status structure is often compromised considerably by the presence of technologically defined jobs that lack clear social identity. Though we all know what a barber is, few of us could immediately identify a "necker" or a "heel seat scourer." [5]

Implications

The foregoing observations lead us to conclude that there exists an intrinsic hiatus between social and physical constraints in any work system. Some physically essential adaptations are always, at some point, either socially undefined or socially deviant; and certain socially prescribed activities are always, at some point, physically irrelevant or even downright disruptive. This situation poses serious problems for the organization of work. Any system of human activities, if it is to be sustained, must be viewed as internally consistent by people performing those activities [6]—yet some activities involved in organized work are inevitably not consistent with one another, but mutually exclusive. If work is to be done, the people performing it must be explicitly oriented to the mutual adaptation of the physical components of the work system; but such physical adaptation cannot occur in a way *actually* thoroughly consistent with social requirements. Therefore, the specific question is: How can the relationship of the work organization to the social setting be culturally defined so that the members of the work organization *perceive* work as part of a consistent system of behavior?

There are two general ways in which such perception is possible. The first is to define culturally only one component of the work system as being related to the setting, thus leaving the other two components free to be adapted to that one component physically without regard to their relationships to the social setting. The second is by internally differentiating the work organization into segregated segments, such that no segment of the work organization is concerned with relationships having contradictory implications. Both of these ways of coping with the situation result, in principle, in members of the work organization viewing work as part of a system of consistent activities. Neither of these patterns, of course, actually resolves the intrinsic dilemma in work. Both represent

---

[5] Wilbert E. Moore, *The Conduct of the Corporation* (New York: Random House, Inc., 1962), p. 44.

[6] A variety of theoretical approaches converge on this position. See for example Claude Lévi-Strauss, *Structural Anthropology*, trans. C. Jacobson and B. G. Schoepf (New York: Basic Books, Inc., Publishers, 1963), pp. 277-323; Leon Festinger, *A Theory of Cognitive Dissonance* (New York: Harper & Row, Publishers, 1957).

merely an accommodation that is institutionally adequate to the continued persistence of organized work. Because a contradiction is still in fact present, both of these "accommodations" have latent consequences. The first entails eventual tension between the work organization and the social setting, because the entire work system is not being adapted to the setting. The second involves eventual strain within the work organization itself, because its segregated parts will ultimately in some respects function at cross purposes. Meanwhile, however, work goes on.

FORMS OF ORGANIZED WORK

The projection of the foregoing line of reasoning against our model outlined in Figure 1.1 results in a typology that distinguishes four basic forms of organized work. In the first place, our model offers three ways in which the work organization can relate only one component of the work system to the social setting, and to relate the other two components physically to the first, without immediate regard to social implications. Either production objectives, technology, or the structure of the work organization itself can be culturally defined as directly related to the social setting. We thus distinguish *production determined, technologically determined,* and *socially determined* work organization, respectively. In our fourth form, which we shall call *pluralistic* work organization, the work organization is internally differentiated in such a way that inconsistency is avoided in the orientation of any given segment of the organization.

These four forms will be found to differ, both in the extent to which each is technically suited to industrial production, and in their differential distribution over various types of nonindustrial societies. This typology is therefore, we believe, more than an exercise in taxonomy, for the capacity of a developing society to develop forms of organized work suited to industrial production would seem to be a critical factor in its modernization. Let us therefore review the most general distinctive characteristics of each of these four types.

Production Determined Work Organizations

A *production determined* work organization is expected to adopt production objectives as given by the social setting. It is then expected to devise, on physical grounds, a technology suited to the achievement of those objectives, and, similarly on physical grounds, to structure itself so as to be able to carry on the technology effectively. Because it is not expected to adapt either the technology or its own structure directly to the social setting, it is free to make the prescribed physical adaptations within the work system without regard to possibly conflicting social constraints. This does not mean that these constraints are absent; on the contrary, as Figure 1.1 has shown, they are always present. What we mean is that the work organization does not take them into primary account in its purposive work behavior.

By the same token, we do not mean to imply that the work organization might not, at some point, give these constraints some attention. Indeed, it may be compelled to do so precisely because they have *not* been taken into account as a part of work per se, and hence emerge as a particularly severe source of strain. Our point is that production determined work organizations are not expected to consider relationships between technology and organization structure, on the one hand, and the social setting, on the other, as part of the work process itself. These relationships may be ignored entirely or may be looked upon as giving rise to problems over which requirements of production determined work take precedence. The over-all effect is that production objectives are taken as given, with technology and organization structure then physically adapted to their achievement without primary regard to the possible social implications of doing so.

Aside perhaps from certain military-related activities in wartime, our own culture seems to provide few examples of production determined work. Plains Indian buffalo hunting, however, provides some striking instances of this type. At certain times of the year, entire communities organized themselves to hunt buffalo. The hunt was a general social goal in that it was culturally defined as part of the yearly round, and not subject to discretion by the community as a work organization. The community, that is, did not decide to do some work, and then decide to hunt, rather than to do some other kind of work. Hunting was simply institutionalized as a community activity. Furthermore, the community typically reorganized itself expressly for the purpose of hunting, with the form of reorganization dictated by technological demands. A special system of roles was instituted and in some cases even enforced by a special police contingent. Persons were assigned to these roles on the basis of known ability, rather than on the basis of age, kinship, or other usual criteria. Frequently an entirely different structure of officialdom is reported for buffalo hunts than for other occasions. Certain general social criteria for role assignment, to be sure, were evident. For example, it usually happened that older people performed different tasks than did young people, and women almost invariably assumed different roles than did men. But such assignments occurred within the context of a broader set of technologically based requirements, rather than the other way around. It is clear that the structure of the technology was adapted to the production objectives, and the organization structure to the technology, primarily on the basis of achieving physical effectiveness, with any social norms and observances that might interfere with such effectiveness suspended for the occasion.[7]

What is the ultimate effect of "suspending" normal cultural expectations in the interest of physical effectiveness under such circumstances? In the case of the particular example given, as with many production determined organizations, no particular problems arose, because the work organization was temporary. When the hunt was over, the usual expectations were resumed. However, production determined work organizations of more permanent duration do present difficulties. Despite the fact that direct relationships between the social setting, on the one hand, and technology and organization structure, on the other, are left undefined culturally, the actual effect of continued physical adaptation without reference to the social setting is a gradual disengagement of the work system from the social setting, and a consequent tendency toward an anomic condition. If social stability is to be maintained under such circumstances, one of three events must occur. First, the work could simply stop. This is, in fact, the most frequent adjustment in production determined situations; the work is usually intermittent, and the organization temporary, as in the example given. Buffalo hunting was not only seasonal, but was not ordinarily continuous even in season. Second, if the work were extremely salient in the social structure, the kinds of organizational patterns it generated could feed back into the social setting and bring about social change. Though this possibility is too intriguing to dismiss, we have been unable to find any empirical instance of its occurrence in production determined work. (Something analogous regularly occurs with technologically determined work, as we shall see.) The third possibility is that discrepancies between the physically adapted organization structure, and what the organization structure would be if it were structured according to general social norms, would become so great as to be visible, and thereby result in direct efforts from the social setting to "bring the work organization back into line." Our empirical data will show that there are conditions under which this does happen, with the important consequence that with direct social pressure the work organization shifts from being production determined to being socially determined.

Thus production determined work organizations are, in principle, related to the social setting only by virtue of their pursuit of culturally given production objectives. They are expected to adapt a technology

[7] Robert H. Lowie, *The Religion of the Crow Indians* (New York: American Museum of Natural History, 1922), pp. 357-59.

to those objectives, and their own structure to the technology, on the basis of criteria of physical effectiveness, without direct regard to social implications. Tensions therefore tend to arise between the organization and its setting, as a result of both its own structure and the technology it is carrying on. Barring the possibility of social change in the setting, such tensions are resolved either because the organization is temporary, or through its change to a socially determined form.

Technologically Determined Work Organizations

Technologically determined work organizations are expected to take, as culturally given, some relatively well-defined external technology, adapt their own structure to its exploitation, and then employ that technology to achieve production objectives. In principle, the necessary physical adaptations are possible because both production objectives and organization structure are left free of direct influence from the social setting. However, the situation is not that simple. Any technology institutionalized as part of the social setting is defined in relatively general terms. In our own culture, for example, we often think of "technology" as a whole as a social institution. The work organization is thus not ordinarily initially faced with any very specific, particular technology, but rather with some generalized body of knowledge and capabilities. Similarly, no particular, specific set of production objectives clearly flows from the situation; a wide variety of production objectives is possible, depending on the particular application of the general technology. The technologically determined work organization is thus especially faced with the problem of decision making. It must decide what objectives to pursue and what its own structure shall be; and it is, by our model, expected to do both of these things on physical technological grounds. The crux of the matter, however, is that to do this is impossible, because the technology is not specific enough to imply directly either any definite set of production objectives or any explicit organization structure. Rather, the technology sets limits to the structure of each of these components. Decisions about their specific content must therefore be made on other than technological grounds.

Two courses of action are open to the technologically determined work organization in making these decisions. Both courses may be pursued simultaneously, or either one may be pursued alone. First, the organization may, on the basis of general social criteria, select various production objectives, and "try" them until it finds one that falls within the physically allowable range of its general technology. It then physically adapts a particular technology to the objective chosen, and its own structure to that particular technology. Second, the organization may alternatively "try" various structures that it could assume in light of general social prescriptions until it finds one that can perform some particular technology consistent with the initial general technological orientation of the organization. It then carries out that technology, and produces whatever that particular technology yields.

The difficulty with both of these procedures is that in order to carry out either one, the work organization must directly consider the relationship of the social setting to some component of the work system in addition to technology. If the first alternative is followed, production objectives are selected on the basis of general social criteria, and if the second alternative is followed, the structure of the work organization itself is similarly selected. The effect in either case is to introduce more than one relationship of the social setting to the work system in the cultural definition of organized work. As a result, the intrinsic inconsistency between physical and social forces tends to become culturally recognized. Technologically determined work organizations are therefore extraordinarily unstable. Whenever they come into being, we would expect them almost immediately to begin to change into some other form. Our model suggests three possibilities. First, if production objectives are the main focus of decision, one might expect a shift to a production determined form. For social developmental reasons, which we shall discuss later and which are exogenous to our model of the work system, this shift is either very rare or nonexistent. Second, if work organization structure is the main focus of decision, the organization might shift to a socially determined form. This, as we shall see, is a very real possibility. Third, if conditions otherwise permit the organization to become internally differentiated, it could become pluralistic. This change is critical to industrial development, and we shall examine the circumstances surrounding it in some detail later.

Because of the extreme instability of this form, it is exceedingly difficult to find "pure" empirical instances of technologically determined work organizations. The typical modern industrial firm, though it is ordinarily pluralistic, resembles a technologically determined work organization in certain respects. It is typically oriented to a general body of technological knowledge and capabilities, and it makes decisions about production objectives as well as its own structure in at least partial light of this technological orientation. Actually, technologically determined work appears as an important transitional form in the course of industrial development, and is thus more accurately a "focus of tendencies" than an organizational type in its own right. Nevertheless, something very close to it may at times be observed in some newly developing areas. Suppose, for example, that a developing country desires, or is politically obliged, to take advantage of opportunities to use foreign technical know-how and investment in a program of "forced draft" industrialization and decides, say, to establish an automobile assembly plant. This country does not have the resources necessary to manufacture parts, so it decides to import all parts from abroad. It likewise does not have the resources to market the cars itself, so it contracts with a foreign company to do that as well. In short, it in effect imports a technology of automobile assembly, essays to adapt a work organization to that technology, and then proceeds to assemble cars. The result could be something very close to a "pure" technologically determined work organization, depending on how the factory work force is recruited. However, the tendencies toward instability are already present. The country has decided to produce cars as a matter of political policy; so the work organization tends toward being production determined. At the same time, it is dependent upon a foreign company for marketing, and over time this dependence could result, among other possibilities, in the social determination of domestic assembly operations. In the face of these two opposing pressures—which in a very real sense hit the work system "from both ends"—the domestic operation is unlikely to remain technologically determined for long, if indeed it ever was. One can also see from this example one reason why a shift to production determined work is unlikely under such circumstances. Such a shift, in this case, would require that domestic political policy win out over foreign investment and still result in continued production of cars, whether they could be sold or not. A much more likely outcome is that either the source of foreign investment would gain control, leaving the domestic operation socially determined (and thereby unsuited to further modernization), or some balance between foreign and domestic control would be struck in the context of a pluralistic organization.[8]

Thus technologically determined work organizations are presumably related to the social setting only through technology; but the inherent decision problems lead to tendencies for other relationships to the social setting to develop, and thus render technologically determined work highly unstable. For all practical purposes it therefore exists only as a transitional form, and tends to move in the direction of either social determination or pluralism.

Socially Determined Work Organizations

Socially determined forms are the simplest of all the four types, and—unfortunately for industrial development—also the most stable. In a so-

[8] I am indebted to Mr. Rafael A. Rodriguez, a student at the Harvard Business School, for this example.

cially determined work organization the structure of the work organization is socially given. Implicit in this structure is some technology, in the sense that when the roles in the organization are performed according to general cultural prescriptions, a technology is carried out. This technology, in turn, results physically in the achievement of some production objective. In the course of pursuing this objective, the work organization is not concerned with the direct relationship of this objective as such to the social setting, nor with the direct relationship of the technology to the social setting. Rather, the organization itself is oriented primarily to the social setting directly, and it "automatically," as it were, performs work as a result of its general social functioning.

A typical example of a socially determined work organization would be a family unit doing agricultural work in a society in which kinship roles, among other things, prescribe such work. Similarly, a work organization recruited by a forced labor system wherein work appears as part of a political obligation would likewise be socially determined. Under some circumstances contractual work also emerges as socially determined, specifically where contractual relations are defined in general terms, with work as one of the obligations they entail.

In principle, socially determined work organizations face problems somewhat analogous to those of production determined forms, in that one might expect the technologies they are carrying out, and the objectives they are pursuing, gradually to become disengaged from the social setting. In practice, however, this tendency is likely to be less marked than one might at first suppose. The fact that the work organization is so intimately tied up with the social setting not only seems automatically to give a certain degree of sanction to whatever it does, but also makes it easier to exert pressure on the work organization to "correct" anything it might be doing in opposition to social norms. Work systems with socially determined organizations are thus considerably more stable than are either production determined or technologically determined forms; they are structured in such a way that any very severe deviations from social norms are immediately extinguished. The difficulties they entail are more on the side of inaction than of overt deviant behavior. For these very reasons, socially determined work organizations are notably lacking in capacity to adapt to certain kinds of social change. If, for example, cultural values shift in the direction of industrialization, and measures are undertaken on the level of national policy to develop industrial production, socially determined work without a previous history of industrial performance will be adaptable to the new technologies only with the severest difficulty, because they are in a very real sense grass roots based.

Socially determined work organizations, then, are related to the social setting directly through the organization structure itself. They therefore tend to function as a stabilizing force in society. Their technological difficulties are those of omission, rather than commission, and these difficulties are felt in the presence of pressures toward change on the level of production objectives and technology. Unlike the two preceding forms, they do not tend to change into any other form.

Pluralistic Work Organizations

Pluralistic work organizations are internally differentiated into segregated subunits, each of which is concerned with a different set of consistent relationships in the work situation, and all of which, taken together, are concerned with all the relationships in the work system and between the work system and the social setting. Pluralistic work organizations are thus qualitatively different from all of the preceding types, precisely because they do succeed in achieving an orientation to all of the relationships between the work system and the social setting. They therefore might appear at first glance to fly in the face of our model. Actually they do not, for they achieve this total orientation because their subunits are specialized and segregated from one another in such a way that the inevitable inconsistencies between the activities of different subunits remain culturally undefined, and hence not immediately visible. For example, one subunit might be concerned with selecting objectives to be pursued in light of cultural values, whereas another subunit might be concerned with choosing technologies with reference to cultural values and identifying objectives that could be pursued by those technologies. Each of those subunits would be internally consistent. By our model, however, both would inevitably at some point operate at cross purposes with the other. For instance, no set of objectives selected by the first subunit will ever completely coincide with any set of objectives developed by the second subunit. The objectives of the first derive directly from the social setting, whereas those of the second derive from the physical implications of the technology. However, since the two subunits concerned are organizationally segregated from one another, this inconsistency does not enter into the cultural definition of the organization and is therefore (in principle) not perceived by the members. Thus, through segregated specialization of subunits, pluralistic work organizations may be culturally defined and perceived as internally consistent, despite the fact that they are not and cannot be.

The typical modern industrial firm is pluralistic, not because it merely contains a variety of specialized subunits, but because the boundaries between specialties are drawn so that, among other things, they by and large preclude any given subunit from being continuously concerned with any set of relationships involving inconsistency between physical and social forces. Thus the marketing and sales unit is oriented to the relationship of the work system (specifically, production objectives) to the social setting, and is not concerned with internal physical relationships in the work system. The latter relationships, on the specific level, are the concern of a unit likely to be called the "production department," which, in turn, is not concerned with any relationships between the work system and the social setting, nor with general technological matters. Similarly, the research and development or engineering unit is involved with the way technology in general relates to the social setting, and the implications of generalized technology for both production objectives and organization structure. It is not, however, concerned with the specific production aspects of technology or with the direct relationship of either production objectives or organization structure to the social setting.[9] The internal concerns of each of these specialized units are consistent with one another; taken together, the concerns of all these units would be inconsistent, in terms of our model. It is this particular kind of specialization, not specialization in general, that identifies pluralistic work organization. Specialization per se is often present, as a matter of fact, in non-pluralistic forms of organized work. However, in such instances it is not derivable from the assumption that it avoids inconsistency between the physical and social aspects of work. Rather, it takes the form of an ordinary technical division of labor, or reflects general social role differentiation, quite independently of our model. Pluralistic work organizations, too, typically entail these types of internal differentiation as well. What makes them pluralistic is that that differentiation, however otherwise elaborate it may be, includes boundaries that segregate contradictory physical and social constraints from one another.

All internally differentiated work organizations, whether pluralistic or not, involve problems of *coordination*, that is, the maintenance of functional coherence among specialized subunits performing unlike, but complementary, activities. Pluralistic work organizations alone have built into themselves internal problems of *integration*, that is, the maintenance of cohesiveness among specialized subunits performing mutually exclusive activities. To be sure, analogous problems exist in other forms of work organization, but they appear as problems in the relationship of the organization to its social setting, and not, in principle, as problems internal to the work organization itself. A central problem, therefore, with pluralistic work organization is the maintenance of integration. One way

[9] See Paul R. Lawrence and Jay W. Lorsch, *Organization and Environment* (Boston: Division of Research, Graduate School of Business Administration, Harvard University, 1967), p. 8.

in which integration is maintained is through the spatial segregation of the subunits to be integrated, so that nobody in any given subunit becomes fully aware of what anyone in another subunit is doing. There are, however, limits to which segregation can function as an integrative device, because in other respects it is obviously inherently divisive. Another important integrative device is managerial ideology. Successful integration depends partly on pluralistic ignorance, but equally on the will to keep trying. As Max Weber puts it, "an organization is a system of *continuous* purposive activity." [10]

We are thus driven to infer that any pluralistic work organization must have some ideology of integration that defines organizational difficulties in terms considerably different from their actual nature, and which, if believed, will result in continued participation despite the fact that the cause is, in a very real sense, always hopeless. It is no accident, for example, that so many problems in modern industrial management are ascribed to "personalities," or "human nature," and that "ability to deal with people" is thought to be both important and "intangible." Unquestionably, a great many organizational difficulties are due to personalities, and few would deny that ability to deal with people effectively is a great asset to any administrator. The point is that even when these contentions do not apply, in view of our model it can be very important for people to believe that they do. Moreover, the continued maintenance of any ideology requires that some of the attributes it specifies forever remain "intangible." Behavior in a pluralistic work organization is thus a combination of continued hopes, however false, with valiant efforts to repair what is ultimately irreparable. Such an organization is, indeed, doomed to be a "system of continuous purposive activity."

We would thus expect problems of differentiation and integration to be present to a unique degree in a pluralistic work organization.[11] Not the least of these problems is the question of exactly how such organizations are differentiated, what kinds and how many subunits are likely to exist, and what aspects of the work system each will be concerned with. Almost limitless variety would seem possible, subject only to the stricture that no one subunit be oriented to relationships that, by our model, are intrinsically inconsistent. However, the practical range of patterns of differentiation is quite limited, owing to the probability that pluralistic organization develops from technologically determined forms. As for integration, we would expect its importance in pluralistic organization to make for a unique emphasis on "management" as such, in which questions

[10] Max Weber, *Wirtschaft und Gesellschaft* (Tübingen: J. C. B. Mohr, 1947), p. 28, italics added.
[11] Lawrence and Lorsch, *op. cit.*, p. 8.

of managerial strategy, buttressed by considerable ideological content, would bulk large.

Our argument up to this point may be summarized as follows:

1. Organized work involves two sets of constraints, physical and social, which are in basic opposition to each other.
2. No work system can therefore be adapted both to physical and social exigencies at the same time.
3. In view of this situation, organized work can be institutionalized in four different ways: as production determined, technologically determined, socially determined, and pluralistic. Each of these four types provides the work organization with a distinctive set of orientations to the work situation through which it can cope with the opposition between physical and social constraints.

What difference does all this make? The remainder of this chapter will attempt to answer that question. The next section will show that we would expect these forms to differ markedly from one another in certain performance characteristics—in effectiveness, efficiency, and innovative capacity—and that these differences have implications for the suitability of one form as opposed to another for industrial production. We shall then argue that certain kinds of societies are more likely to exhibit one form of organized work as opposed to another; that for this reason the process of social development may be expected to affect organized work; and, finally, that the over-all system of causal relationships between social structure and organized work has implications for the transition from traditional to modern industrial society.

EFFECTIVENESS, EFFICIENCY, AND INNOVATIVE CAPACITY

By *effectiveness* we mean the simple capacity of a work organization to carry on a given kind of technology. *Efficiency* is the minimization of organizational activity relative to physical output, holding constant the degree of technological sophistication. *Innovative capacity* is the capacity to make decisions resulting in the adaptation of the organization to changing conditions. These three performance characteristics are likely to be of considerable importance in any work situation, and they assume particular significance in modern industrial work. Not all kinds of organization are effective in carrying on industrial production. Furthermore, modern industrial production is impossible without some minimal emphasis on efficiency. To be sure, efficiency cannot be the only value in any society, and perhaps it can never be even the most important value. By the same token, no industrial economy can function if organizational activity per se is allowed to take precedence at all points over actual production, particularly in an internationally competitive situation. Similarly, the capacity to innovate is of particular importance in an industrial economy, not only because of frequent shifts in market situations, but because social change generally is relatively rapid. It is important, therefore, that organizations carrying on modern industrial work be relatively efficient, and capable of considerable innovation.

Effectiveness

The differences in the ways in which the four organizational types are constrained to operate lead us to expect them to differ markedly from one another in range of effectiveness, efficiency, and innovative capacity. As regards effectiveness, we would expect production determined, technologically determined, and pluralistic organizations to be capable in principle of carrying on any technology. In contrast, we would expect socially determined organizations to be quite restricted in their range of possible effectiveness. The reason for this limitation is that the former three types are all defined as being directly adaptable to technological exigencies, whereas socially determined organizations are not. Rather, their structures are directly prescribed socially without regard to technological exigencies, and are consequently strictly speaking not *adaptable* to any technology. They thus cannot perform any kind of work not already imbedded in some system of social roles. Large-scale technologies requiring vast numbers of people and a highly complex division of labor, especially, present problems for socially determined organizations; the number of persons present and the number of roles differentiated cannot, in socially determined organizations, exceed the maximum number given in the social setting, regardless of technological exigencies. A corollary of our hypothesis, therefore, is that socially determined work organizations, except perhaps very small businesses, are in particular not well adapted to modern industrial production. Their range of possible effectiveness, especially in highly complex technological situations, is too limited.

Efficiency

By a similar line of reasoning, we would also expect socially determined work organizations to have problems with efficiency. Because their members are oriented both to the immediate work situation and to the social setting, role content is at best split between work per se and other social considerations. It is hence impossible for members to work without also giving attention to non-work activities; indeed, the latter are likely to overshadow the former to the point where work itself becomes a by-product of a broader social situation. We would therefore expect socially determined work organizations to be relatively inefficient. Production determined and technologically determined work organizations present a sharp contrast on this score. Relationships between organization and social setting are left culturally undefined, so the organization is left free to be governed solely by technological considerations, and can thus presumably attain a high level of efficiency. Pluralistic work organizations would seem to present a mixed picture, depending on precisely how they are structured. As a whole, they inevitably entail significant amounts of non-work activity. However, it is not inevitable that each member, in his capacity as member, will be obliged to perform activities unrelated to work, as is the case with socially determined forms. The tendency is, rather, for entire organizational subunits to be specialized as between work and social support functions. As a result we would expect work per se to be conducted highly efficiently, and the question to arise as to what else the organization is supposed to be doing, rather than how efficiently the work is conducted. The problem of efficiency in pluralistic work organization is thus complicated by the organization's tendency to develop multiple outputs, many of which can in themselves be separately subjected to some calculus of efficiency. Over-all, we would therefore expect pluralistic organizations to be somewhat less efficient than production determined or technologically determined forms, but considerably more efficient than socially determined types, which lack the capacity for output specialization and consequently cannot control what, in an economic analysis, would emerge as their operating costs.

Innovative Capacity

Both socially determined and production determined work organizations lack innovative capacity, because neither has occasion to develop any very complex decision-making structure. The former, indeed, are expected to make essentially no decisions, but rather to operate simply through a predetermined set of roles. The latter are expected to make some technological-adaptive decisions, but are not expected to make decisions about what objectives to pursue. Technologically determined and pluralistic work organizations are, on the other hand, expected to make not only technological-adaptive decisions, but also decisions as to what objectives to pursue and how to move from general to specific levels of technology. They are thus under some pressure to develop complex, innovative decisional machinery.

Summary

The foregoing discussion is summarized by Table 1.1. It seems evident

Table 1.1

Theoretically Expected Effectiveness, Efficiency, and Innovative Capacity of Work Organizations

Type of organization	Effectiveness	Efficiency	Innovative capacity
Production determined	High	High	Low
Socially determined	Low	Low	Low
Technologically determined	High	High	High
Pluralistic	High	Fairly High	High

that socially determined work organization is ill-suited to modern industrial production, especially on a large scale. From the standpoint of effectiveness it faces problems of supplying adequate manpower and adequate role differentiation. It is almost certain to be rather inefficient, and it lacks decisional and innovative capacity. Production determined forms seem somewhat better off in these respects, though they still lack innovative and decisional capacity. Technologically determined and pluralistic work organizations appear to be the best suited for modern industrial work. They are relatively efficient, and they are constrained to operate in ways conducive to the development of decisional and innovative capacity.

These hypotheses, if they are correct, imply that societies about to embark upon industrialization will be able to do so most successfully if they have the capacity to support technologically determined or pluralistic work organization. Production determined work is also a theoretical possibility. However, it would appear that societies characterized generally by socially determined work would encounter difficult organizational problems in the transition to industrialism. Bearing these implications in mind, let us now turn to a consideration of the effects of social development on organized work. In particular, What kinds of work organization would traditional societies, on the eve of industrialization, be most likely to exhibit?

SOCIAL DEVELOPMENT, THE DEVELOPMENT
OF ORGANIZED WORK, AND INDUSTRIALIZATION

"Social development" is a rather difficult concept. The overly sweeping formulations of the earlier "classical" social evolutionists have not been entirely forgotten, and as a result of their legacy many theories of social development today have an annoying tendency to be both incorrect and in serious disrepute. Yet, social development is a topic that the study of modernization cannot avoid, and the literature on modernization is replete with at least implicit ideas about developmental patterns. As a minimum, it is possible to state certain general conditions that are either requisite or prerequisite to industrialism, on both theoretical and empirical grounds.[12] The task is, furthermore, made easier by the fact that it is possible to keep the argument on a fairly gross level and still find something out. In all societies that have become industrialized, for example, sedentary agriculture has been well established. Similarly, all such societies possess some form of centralized government. In addition, it is commonly agreed that a fairly high degree of commercialization, as well as a geographically mobile labor force, are among the conditions essential to industrialization.

One can proceed beyond this point by examining each of these requisite conditions, and asking what other conditions are either requisite or prerequisite to them in turn. Certain kinds of property systems, for example, appear to be requisite to sedentary agriculture. In addition, these conditions may in themselves tend to generate consequences that might include further conditions essential to industrialization, and so forth. The result of such a line of reasoning is a conceptualization of the direction in which societies that become industrialized develop. It is not necessarily a theory of social development, because the causal mechanisms are at best not fully specified. It does not therefore allege that all, or even most, societies possessing these conditions move inexorably toward industrialization. It merely asserts that if they do, they do so in terms of a particular series of events. One can validly observe, for instance, that sedentary agriculture is essential to centralized government, or that centralized government is essential to commercialization, without specifying exactly how centralized government or commercialization comes into being. The form of the argument is that if certain circumstances are present upon the random arrival of some trait, that trait will be adopted by the society.

[12] For a discussion of the concepts *requisite* and *prerequisite* see Marion J. Levy, Jr., *The Structure of Society* (Princeton, N.J.: Princeton University Press, 1952), pp. 39-45.

The resultant scheme, though it does specify direction and some causation, can in this way be explicitly left open. One can, in this manner, examine the relationship between social development and organized work without committing oneself to a particular theory of social development in detail.

This is the general strategy we shall follow. It will not, at our hands, yield a theory of development, but will enable us to classify primitive and traditional societies according to how closely they resemble modern industrial societies in certain given respects. We can then examine the implications of the traits possessed by each type of society for organized work, and thus formulate some hypotheses about what forms of organized work are likely to be characteristic of each type of society. In this way we shall at least be able to estimate whether, when societies move in the direction of industrialism on the level of general social structure, they at the same time tend to generate forms of organized work likewise progressively better adapted to industrial production.

Preindustrial Social Development

What social structural traits are prerequisite to industrial society? What are the prerequisites of these traits? What subsequent conditions do these traits tend to cause? These are the questions on which we shall now focus, but we will not try to answer them completely. We simply wish to know enough about preindustrial development to help us predict something about organized work. The traits we have selected have thus been chosen with a view to their relevance to organized work in particular, rather than to social development generally, and are restricted to those on which cross-cultural data are widely available. Because there is a dearth of theory as to how social development relates to organized work, we shall keep our scheme as simple as possible.

We shall begin with the observation—in a formal sense, the assumption—that both sedentary agriculture (planned cultivation of crops on fixed plots of land in settled communities) and centralized government (the presence of a legitimate political group exercising control over several geographically distinct communities) are essential prerequisites to industrialization. What further prerequisites would we expect these prerequisites to entail?

Sedentary agriculture and exclusive proprietorship. As a means of food production, sedentary agriculture is unique in its dependence upon certain stringent beliefs and practices concerning real property. While land is under cultivation, it is essentially impossible for it to be used for any other purpose. The existence of sedentary agriculture therefore depends on a property system that guarantees that given tracts of land remain continuously and predictably accessible for agricultural use alone. Comparative study reveals that apart from a few unique and rather exotic instances, the only way in which this pattern of land use is consistently institutionalized is through the vesting of continuous rights to specific tracts in particular social units. Such a system of tenure, which we shall call *exclusive proprietorship*, is thus a necessary condition for the existence of sedentary agriculture, for all practical purposes. Exclusive proprietorship does not, however, *cause* sedentary agriculture; it is merely an essential condition for it. Thus, in addition to societies exhibiting neither of these two characteristics, we would expect to discover societies with exclusive proprietorship but without sedentary agriculture, as well as societies having both. However, we would anticipate that no stable society practicing sedentary agriculture would be found without exclusive proprietorship.

Centralized government. Where and how does centralized government fit into this picture? In common with other relatively elaborate institutional arrangements, centralized government cannot flourish save in a society sufficiently removed from the subsistence level to permit the allocation of time and energy to the maintenance of complex social arrangements not directly involved in food production.[13] It is on this basis that we argue that sedentary agriculture is itself ordinarily a necessary prerequisite to centralized government. Sedentary agriculture represents a major technological improvement in food production. Few societies that do not practice it are able, if they are to survive, to devote a sufficient proportion of their time and energy to sustain any structure so institutionally complex as a centralized government. Furthermore, the combination of exclusive proprietorship with sedentary agriculture would seem likely to set mechanisms in motion that themselves would tend to produce centralized government. The growing importance, and probable eventual indispensability, of agriculture as a source of food means that tillable land becomes an increasingly scarce resource in growing demand. As a result, those social units exercising control over landed property tend to assume increasing political importance. This process is apt to be accelerated, too, by population growth resulting from the enhanced effectiveness of food production. Such growth further emphasizes inequalities

[13] For various discussions of this general line of reasoning, see V. Gordon Childe, *Man Makes Himself* (New York: New American Library, 1951); Leslie H. White, *The Evolution of Culture* (New York: McGraw-Hill Book Company, 1959); Julian H. Steward, *et al., Irrigation Civilizations* (Washington: Pan American Union, 1955); Otis Dudley Duncan, "Social Organization and the Ecosystem," in *Handbook of Modern Sociology*, ed. Robert E. Faris (Chicago: Rand McNally & Co., 1964), Chap. 2; Martin Orans, "Surplus," *Human Organization*, 25 (1966), 24-32.

in property distribution, and thus combines with the other forces discussed to lay a powerful basis for political centralization. Whether or not such centralization actually occurs is doubtless dependent upon the further presence of a variety of cultural values and other social conditions. Without the possibility of at least a near monopoly of control over scarce resources, however, it is doubtful that stable central political control could appear. Conceivably, centralized political power might be supported through control over some scarce resource other than landed property—we shall, in fact, see that this occasionally happens—but alternatively possible resources do not seem empirically to appear so consistently or powerfully. Sedentary agriculture in combination with exclusive proprietorship will therefore, in all probability, not only be a necessary condition for, but will actually tend to lead to, the development of a centralized political system. Some, but not all, societies with sedentary agriculture will thus possess centralized governments, but almost no society with centralized government will fail to exhibit sedentary agriculture, if our argument is correct.

Complex stratification systems. What further developments might we expect to arise from the combination of exclusive proprietorship, sedentary agriculture, and centralized government? This combination provides a strong foundation for hierarchical social differentiation. It does not inevitably produce such differentiation, but preindustrial society presents few empirical instances of other, equally powerful and stable bases of social hierarchy. We thus conclude that some societies with centralized government will also possess *complex stratification systems,* that is, social hierarchies consisting of three or more differentiated classes or castes culturally defined on some basis other than kinship,[14] but that virtually every society having a complex stratification system will also possess a centralized government.

"Primitive" versus "traditional" society. The preceding argument suggests that exclusive proprietorship is essential to sedentary agriculture, which, in turn, is essential to centralized government, which, in turn, is essential to a complex stratification system. If this is true we would expect preindustrial societies to fit a rough scale of social development, relative to industrialization, with five types of preindustrial society: 1) societies possessing none of the traits discussed; 2) societies exhibiting exclusive proprietorship only; 3) societies with both exclusive proprietorship and sedentary agriculture; 4) societies with exclusive proprietorship, sedentary agriculture, and centralized government; and 5) societies with all four characteristics: exclusive proprietorship, sedentary agriculture,

[14] George P. Murdock, "World Ethnographic Sample," *American Anthropologist,* 59 (1957), 673.

centralized government, and complex stratification systems. Type 1 would be the furthest removed from industrialism; type 5 would be the closest to it. To the extent that a society is closer to type 1, we shall call it a *primitive* society, and to the extent that a nonindustrial society is closer to type 5, we shall call it a *traditional* society.

The Development of Organized Work

The question now arises as to whether we would expect societies that most closely resemble industrial societies also to exhibit forms of work organization most readily adaptable to industrial production. We have already seen that socially determined work organization is least adaptable to industrial work, technologically determined and pluralistic forms are most suited to industrial production, and production determined organizations fall somewhere in between. Thus if the development of work organization is consistent with general social development, we would expect to find a movement from socially determined work through production determined to technologically determined and pluralistic forms as one moves from primitive to traditional society.

"Primitive" work. But this is not what happens, nor would we anticipate it theoretically. Moreover, this situation poses serious problems for industrialization, at least for organized work.

Let us look at our scale of preindustrial social development, and see what implications its traits have for organized work. In the first place, societies that do not practice sedentary agriculture are apt to be very close to the level of subsistence. This fact has three implications. First, most of the work carried on in such societies will necessarily be directed toward food production. Second, because food production occupies so much attention, it is not only very likely to be culturally defined as a general social goal but will also have to be highly effective if the society is to survive. Third, very elaborate social arrangements, which might technically interfere with the food quest, will not be possible.

These considerations suggest that organized work in highly primitive societies would be production determined. Production objectives tend to be defined as general social goals; effectiveness and efficiency have high survival value; and the necessary institutional basis for socially determined work tends to be absent. Such work, furthermore, could not be technologically determined nor pluralistic, for again the necessary institutional bases are lacking; for one thing, no generalized body of technological knowledge and capability exists in highly primitive settings as a specialized segment of culture.

"Traditional" work. Turning now to more traditional societies, we

would expect the course of preindustrial social development to lead to forms of organized work further removed from, rather than closer to, forms suited to industrial production. Traditional societies, like primitive societies, provide no institutional basis for technologically determined or pluralistic forms. They have no generalized, coherent systems of science and technology. It is also doubtful whether, in most traditional societies, work organizations would be large enough to make pluralism possible. Pluralistic work organization requires a large, dispersed membership, with discontinuities in interaction patterns. To be sure, technologically determined organizations perhaps do not, but they do require a generalized technological institutional system. Furthermore, we have seen that technologically determined work organizations are highly unstable, in any event.

On the other hand, socially determined forms not only are particularly well suited to traditional society, but also seem likely to be generated by the process of preindustrial social development itself at the expense of production determined forms. As society moves away from the subsistence level, more resources become available for social development and institutional elaborations, including those surrounding the organization of work. Socially determined work organization thus becomes a possibility. But it is more than just a possibility. The advent of sedentary agriculture tends to produce an over-all dependence upon landed property for food supply. As a result, much work centers on landed property. It is impossible to conceive that under such circumstances the combination of exclusive proprietorship with sedentary agriculture would not produce a tendency for proprietary parties to exert a direct social influence on work organization. This tendency is, furthermore, aided and abetted by the internal tendency of production determined work organizations themselves to become socially determined. With the advent of centralized government and complex stratification, we would also anticipate that influences toward socially determined work would be strengthened.

Adaptability to industrial production. We thus conclude that the course of preindustrial development leads to a decreasing prevalence of production determined work and an increasing prevalence of socially determined work. No tendencies in traditional society that we have as yet identified would make for either technologically determined or pluralistic forms. As we have seen, we would expect technologically determined or pluralistic work organization to be characteristic, if not essential, to modern industrial production. However, the prevailing trend in preindustrial social development would seem to be away from, rather than toward, organizational forms adapted to physical technology. Societies that in other respects most nearly resemble modern industrial society appear to possess forms of organized work that least resemble what is found in modern industry.

CONCLUSIONS AND HYPOTHESES

Our analysis in this chapter of the nature of organized work, the course of preindustrial social development, and the relationships we would expect between the two leaves us with a variety of hypotheses to be investigated and questions to be answered. Our summary here will indicate the order in which they will be considered and developed in the chapters to follow.

First, we shall wish to find out whether our proposed scale of preindustrial social development is realistic. If it proves to be so, we shall then be able to test the following hypotheses:

1. The course of preindustrial social development results in a shift from production determined to socially determined work, with both technologically determined and pluralistic work remaining absent from preindustrial society.

2. Socially determined work organizations have a narrower range of possible effectiveness, are less efficient, and exhibit less capacity for innovation than do production determined work organizations.

3. Therefore, the course of preindustrial social development militates against the development of forms of work organization that would be progressively more suited to industrial production.

Chapter Two will be devoted to a consideration of these hypotheses. If they are confirmed, they raise the question as to how a shift is brought about from socially determined forms of work organization to technologically determined and pluralistic forms of work. Chapter Three will explore this question, and we shall see that the answers we propose in turn have implications for problems of work organization in modern industrial society. Chapters Four and Five will be concerned with these implications, and will additionally consider questions we have already raised about the structure and functioning of pluralistic work organizations.

Let us now assess the reality of the assumptions we have made, test the hypotheses we have proposed, and further explore their implications, by examining some comparative data. A sample of 125 preindustrial societies was drawn according to the criteria set forth by Murdock for his "World Ethnographic Sample," and distributed as evenly as was possible over the six world regions he designates.[1] From the ethnographic literature on each of these societies, material was abstracted bearing on those general social structural dimensions we have discussed, together with information on 359 work organizations, described in varying detail, and distributed approximately equally over the 125 societies. A discussion of details of method, as well as of this general approach and its problems, appears in the Appendix. Owing to unevenness of data, not all 125 societies, or all 359 work organizations, could be used in all phases of the analysis, as the subsequent presentation will indicate.

PREINDUSTRIAL SOCIAL DEVELOPMENT

Our rather simple social development scheme involves four structural characteristics: exclusive proprietorship, sedentary agriculture, centralized government, and complex stratification. We have argued that exclusive proprietorship is requisite to sedentary agriculture; that the combination

CHAPTER TWO

[1] George P. Murdock, "World Ethnographic Sample," *American Anthropologist*, 59 (1957), 664-87.

Organized Work in Preindustrial Society

of exclusive proprietorship with sedentary agriculture is very likely to be requisite to centralized government; and that the combination of all three of these characteristics is conducive to the development of complex stratification. If this argument is correct, preindustrial societies should fit a rough scale. We would expect to find some without any of these four characteristics, some with exclusive proprietorship only, some with exclusive proprietorship and sedentary agriculture, others with exclusive proprietorship, sedentary agriculture, and centralized government, and still others with all four characteristics. On the whole, we would not expect to find other combinations of these characteristics, though the fact that our argument at some points allows for the possibility of structural alternatives suggests that we might anticipate some exceptions.

Table 2.1 indicates that our sample of societies essentially fits this scheme, with 17 exceptions, which we have assimilated to the scale as indicated. The particular societies assigned to each category are shown in the Appendix. The nine exceptional cases without exclusive proprietorship offer unique alternative modes of maintaining the integrity of agricultural land, and, in some instances, do indeed give the impression of

Table 2.1

Developmental Types of Preindustrial Societies

Type	Characteristics present	Characteristics absent	Frequency
I	None	Exclusive proprietorship Sedentary agriculture Centralized government Complex stratification	12
II	Exclusive proprietorship	Sedentary agriculture Centralized government Complex stratification	12
III	Exclusive proprietorship Sedentary agriculture	Centralized government Complex stratification	42 *
IV	Exclusive proprietorship Sedentary agriculture Centralized government	Complex stratification	34 **
V	Exclusive proprietorship Sedentary agriculture Centralized government Complex stratification	None	25
	Total societies		125

* *Includes nine societies without exclusive proprietorship.*
** *Includes eight societies without sedentary agriculture.*

being somewhat unstable in this respect. The eight societies where sedentary agriculture itself is absent all have seacoast fishing economies under very advantageous conditions, the fish providing a more than adequate food supply. Fishing thus operates as a structural substitute for agriculture in producing the effects alleged by our model.

We thus conclude that our conceptual scheme, though crude, is probably basically realistic. At the very least it yields a typology of societies in which some types are clearly closer to conditions essential to industrialization than are other types. On this score, our hypothesis was for the most part couched in terms of necessary but not sufficient conditions, and not in terms of a sequence in which characteristics actually develop. Perhaps they do develop in the sequence in which they occur on the scale. Or maybe they develop in some other way. Centralized government, for example, might well come into being quite independently of any of the items on the scale, and bring with it sedentary agriculture and exclusive proprietorship simultaneously, possibly as a result of their imposition by political power. To be sure, such an event would seem to be improbable, owing to the difficulty of establishing an adequate basis for political power in the absence of a combination of exclusive proprietorship and sedentary agriculture (or some other activity involving an effective monopoly over the control of essential resources). However, our data alone by no means exclude this possibility, or, for that matter, similar possibilities. The point is, though, that for present purposes we do not need to know exactly how social development takes place. It probably can occur in a wide variety of ways, and in various directions. All we need to be able to do is to describe the context that social development provides for organized work, relative to industrialization. It is thus not important whether the four structural characteristics we have identified develop in some definite sequence, or whether some of them develop simultaneously, or whether both possibilities obtain under different circumstances. However they may develop, they result in the pattern indicated by our scale because of their requisite structures, and for this reason, some preindustrial societies more nearly fulfill the social conditions essential for industrialization than do others. In this sense we can use the scale to measure the presumed degree of development, or "proximity to industrialization," present in primitive and traditional society.[2]

---

[2] For a comment on the problem of inferring developmental sequences inductively from Guttman scale patterns, see the author's "Dynamic Inferences from Static Data," *Ameriacn Journal of Sociology*, 70 (1965), 625-27.

SOCIAL DEVELOPMENT AND TYPE OF
WORK ORGANIZATION

In Chapter One we argued that as we move from primitive to traditional society, we would expect to find a decrease in the prevalence of production determined work, and an increase in the prevalence of socially determined work. The relatively unitary goal structure of primitive societies is conducive to production determined organization, and proximity to the subsistence level inhibits sufficiently elaborate institutional support for socially determined forms. Conversely, traditional societies have goal structures that are too diversified and diffuse for production determined work, but at the same time offer sufficiently elaborate institutional structures to support socially determined forms. Furthermore, each of the four items in our scale represents an increase over the preceding one in the degree to which one would expect proprietary parties to exert control over work organization independently of the immediate members of the organization. Exclusive proprietorship itself provides a basis for control over resources and the means of production by social units that are themselves in principle technologically independent of any work system. Sedentary agriculture would intensify such control, because the most important resource involved in exclusive proprietorship is land, and as agriculture becomes increasingly indispensable as a source of food, the status of proprietorship in land becomes increasingly important in work systems. Centralized government and complex stratification both represent further consolidations of power inherent in landed proprietorship, the possibility of its more systematic exercise, and enhanced bases for its diffusion to types of work other than agriculture.

One would additionally expect this entire process to be abetted by mechanisms internal to the work system, arising from its intrinsic inconsistencies. Production determined work is characterized by continuing physical adaptation of the work organization to technology without regard to the actual but culturally undefined relationship of the organization to the social setting. If physical and social forces are, as we have supposed, inherently inconsistent in the work system, such a situation would result through time in increasing discrepancies between the actual organization structure and what the organization structure would be socially expected to be if anyone were paying attention to it. One may reasonably surmise that eventually the magnitude of such discrepancies would render them increasingly visible and hence attract explicit attention. There is thus a tendency toward interplay between the work organization and its setting, which virtually assures that pressures toward change will be brought to bear on the work organization. Visible discrepancies between the work organization and its social setting will be met by efforts from the latter to "bring the organization back into line," resulting in direct pressures toward social determination.

We thus conclude that the greater the degree of preindustrial social development, the less the prevalence of production determined forms, and the greater the prevalence of socially determined forms. We also conclude that because prolonged interplay with the setting would tend to lead to their social determination, observed production determined organizations would tend to be temporary, whereas socially determined work organizations would tend to be permanent.

Method of Classifying Organizations

The 359 work organizations in our sample were classified as pluralistic, socially determined, production determined, or technologically determined by the following procedure. First, the sample was searched to find internally differentiated work organizations in which any subgroup visibly and continuously performed activities inconsistent with those of any other subgroup. The intention was to classify such organizations as pluralistic, regardless of other considerations. As expected, no clearly pluralistic organizations were found in this preindustrial sample, although nine socially determined organizations, to which we shall return in some detail later, did exhibit marked tendencies toward differentiation along pluralistic lines. The sample was then searched to discover socially determined organizations. If organizational relationships among a majority of members were defined by roles held in some other social unit of which they were also members in common, the organization was classified as socially determined. Typical examples would be those in which kinship or political roles also consistently define relationships in a work organization. In applying this criterion, however, general role differentiation on the ubiquitous bases of age, sex, and territoriality as such was excluded.

The remaining organizations were presumed to be either production determined or technologically determined. If decisions as to what objectives to pursue were not made by the organization itself, it was classified as production determined. Many, though not all, primitive hunting organizations fit this criterion. They are not socially determined, and the decision as to whether members should hunt or do some other kind of work is made externally to the work organization itself, usually on the basis of general social norms or as a function of the political system.

It was our intention to classify all organizations that were not pluralistic or socially determined as technologically determined, if they were reported as choosing their production objectives from among a family of alternative possibilities. No clear cases of technologically determined organizations emerged in the present sample, though other instances of such organizations will be indicated in later parts of the book.

The actual classification was done by the author and an independent observer; problems of reliability and methods of resolving differences of judgment are described in the Appendix. Of the 359 cases, 338 proved to be quite readily classifiable. Of the remaining cases, 7, which were obviously either production determined or socially determined but not clearly one or the other, were conservatively classified as production determined, because they appeared in quite highly traditional societies. Ten other similarly doubtful cases were classified as socially determined, inasmuch as no unequivocally clear cases of technological determination were found anywhere in the sample. These 10 cases included the 9 organizations previously identified as having possibly pluralistic tendencies. The 4 cases remaining were dropped from the analysis as unclassifiable. The result was a grand total of 355 work organizations, 96 of which were classified as production determined, 259 as socially determined, and none as technologically determined or pluralistic. In 10 cases, however, as we have seen, the organization might have been technologically determined, and 9 of these cases involved possibly pluralistic tendencies.

Tests of Hypotheses

Type of society and type of work organization. Table 2.2 shows the distribution of type of work organization over scale type of society, and is strikingly consistent with our hypothesis. With preindustrial social development comes a progressive decline in the prevalence of production

Table 2.2

Type of Society and Type of Work Organization

| | Type of Work Organization | |
Type of society	Production determined	Socially determined
I	31	2
II	15	11
III	28	86
IV	22	82
V	0	78

determined work organization, and a progressive increase in the prevalence of socially determined work organization.

Type of work organization and permanence. Table 2.3 shows the relationship between type of work organization and permanence. It too is

Table 2.3

Type of Work Organization and Permanence

Type of work organization	Permanence	
	Temporary	Permanent
Production determined	75	21
Socially determined	0	258

strikingly consistent with expectations; production determined organizations tend to be temporary, and socially determined organizations tend to be permanent. This finding suggests some revision in the inferences we have drawn from our model; in producing more permanent forms of organized work, preindustrial social development would seem in at least this respect to bring work organization closer to industrial norms. However, if our other inferences withstand empirical scrutiny, it also appears that such permanence is not gained without considerable cost.

OPERATING STRUCTURE

Let us now examine, in light of our data, the differences between production determined and socially determined forms that our model leads us to expect. The first of these differences is that of basic operating structure. According to our model, production determined organizations adapt themselves directly to physical exigencies independently of social considerations, whereas socially determined organizations are structured according to social considerations without regard to physical suitability. A direct test of this inference would require detailed data on decisional processes for each type of organization—data we do not have. We can, however, test it indirectly by examining both the nature of the social base of each type of organization and the implications of variations in this base for variations in organizational performance.

The *social base* of a work organization is the social unit from which its membership is drawn. The members of any work organization must come from somewhere, so all work organizations regardless of type will have some social base. In the case of production determined work organizations, we would expect the social base to be rather ill-defined, with variations having little or no effect on actual operations. In the case of socially determined work organizations, however, we would expect the social base to be a rather precisely defined unit whose nature would have considerable effect on operations.

These expectations are largely substantiated by our data. In 62 of the 96 production determined organizations studied, the exact social base proved rather difficult to pin down, beyond the fact that members were drawn from the same general geographical area. Participation proved to be essentially individualistic and voluntary. By "voluntary" we mean the absence of any peculiarly social mechanism compelling participation; not that failure to participate might not result in severe personal deprivations. Indeed, in some cases, repeated failure to participate would almost certainly result in death by starvation. Participation is itself expected only on grounds of individual self-defined self-interest, however, with the result that the organization is presumably freed, as predicted, from built-in systems of interpersonal relationships derived from prior institutionalized associations. Furthermore, the remaining 34 production determined organizations appeared to be essentially similar, although it happened that in each of these cases all of the members came from some readily identifiable group. In 10 instances, the community as a whole seemed to be involved in the work; in 20 cases, participation seemed to be limited to some household; and in 4 instances, participation was limited to some other group within the community. In none of these cases did participation occur *because* of such membership; that is, the work was not in itself part of the role obligations of membership in any of these groups. Some members of the social base group participated in the work; others did not, with no apparent social differences between the participators and the nonparticipators. The fact that the social base was relatively identifiable seems to have been nothing more than an ecological accident. This impression is confirmed by the fact that no significant differences were found between the social base of production determined organizations and any of the various performance characteristics that we shall study presently.

The characteristics of production determined organizations are predictable from technology to the same degree, irrespective of any variations in social base. Furthermore, the 33 production determined organizations having more or less readily identifiable social bases do not differ in any other respect from the 62 without clear social bases. In short, it proved impossible to predict variations in the organizational characteristics of production determined forms from variations in social base, or for that matter in the entire social setting. Our model would lead us to expect precisely this negative result.

The Copper Eskimos provide some very good examples of the rather vague nature of the social base of production determined organization. Specifically, the social base among the Copper Eskimos appears to vary throughout the year, depending on what kinds of hunting and fishing are currently in season. The variations seem clearly to be technologically based. A large number of people are involved in hunting seals during the winter, and at that season the Copper Eskimos tend to live in large communities by the sea. During the summer, though, with the advent of fresh water fishing and hunting possibilities, the communities break up into smaller bands and move inland. The exact social boundaries between bands are not clear, except that members of the same family rarely join different bands. Lake fishers and caribou hunters are drawn from these bands, simply because hunting is considered necessary and men who are around are expected to do it. As the season progresses, the exigencies of deer hunting demand smaller groups, and a further fragmentation into smaller bands occurs. This fragmentation is frequently, though not always, reported as occurring along family lines. Both Jenness and Stefansson report rational and technological answers to questions as to how the hunting occurs and how the groups are constituted. Actual techniques are quite constant among different bands, but the composition of hunting and fishing groups is fairly variable socially, apart from general division of labor by sex, and fluctuates throughout the yearly round according to the kinds of game being hunted and the type of fishing being done.[3]

Socially Determined Organizations

Socially determined work organizations present a sharp contrast. All of them recruit their members from some readily identifiable pre-existing

[3] Diamond Jenness, *The Life of the Copper Eskimos* (Ottawa: F. A. Acland, 1922), pp. 89-91, 116-23; Viljálmur Stefánsson, *The Stefánsson-Anderson Arctic Expedition of the American Museum: Preliminary Ethnological Report,* Anthropological Papers of the American Museum of Natural History, XIV, Pt. 1 (New York, 1914), 21-30, 54-57, 70.

social group or category whose roles include, among other things, an obligation to work. We may distinguish three types of socially determined work organization, according to social base: *familial, political,* and *contractual.*

Familial organizations. Membership in *familial* work organizations is derived from membership in some kinship unit, with participation institutionalized as an obligation of kinship. Such organizations are thus necessarily rather restricted in size, but offer more flexibility on this score than one might imagine through frequent reciprocity arrangements with other families residing in neighboring households. The Buka of the Solomon Islands present a typical example. Each kindred has its own garden property, which is subdivided into family plots. In general, each family works its own plot, though various kinds of communal and sharing arrangements are possible within the kindred. At periods of peak work load, families reciprocate with each other, as well as with families in other kindreds.[4] Familial organizations are thus relatively adaptable to operations of up to moderate scale, but are too small for really large-scale production. Eighty-nine familial organizations appear in our sample.

Political organizations. Political work organizations are based on the institutionalized authority of some person or group to compel others, independently of kinship obligations and by force if necessary, to participate in work. Inasmuch as political relationships are apt to be rather diffuse in traditional society, this type of work organization can be and often is very large. Political work organizations vary considerably in form. Some are based on serfdom or slavery, as in medieval Europe and the ante-bellum southern United States. Others are based on debt peonage, a form relatively more common in the Eastern Hemisphere. In traditional Cambodia, for example, it was common to work off debts in the service of creditors, and not uncommon for a person to suffer lifetime debt peonage, especially in view of interest rates of 200 per cent annually compounded every six months. Chinese usurers would not only make advances in cash but also force the farmers to buy from them and sell to them, thus assuring political control over the work force.[5] An often somewhat less severe form—in the sense that it does not entail continuous service—is the corvée, whereby top political officials can command work in their own interest or deemed to be in the public interest, not unlike a military draft.

---

[4] Walter G. Ivens, *The Island Builders of the Pacific* (London: Seeley, Service, 1930), pp. 267-70; Walter G. Ivens, *Melanesians of the Southeast Solomon Islands* (London: Kegan Paul, Trench, Trubner, 1927), pp. 355-59; Beatrice Blackwood, *Both Sides of Buka Passage* (Oxford: Clarendon Press, 1935), pp. 298-301.

[5] Pierre Gourou, *Land Utilization in French Indo-China,* trans. S. Haden Guest, Elizabeth A. Clark, and Karl J. Pelzer (Washington: Institute of Pacific Relations, 1945), pp. 384-87, 561-62.

We shall not distinguish these various subtypes of political work organization in most of our analysis. We include them here only to illustrate something of the possible range of variation of this form. Eighty-three political work organizations of all types appear in our sample.

Contractual organizations. In contrast to both of the preceding types, participation in *contractual* work organizations is based on an explicit agreement to behave in a specified way for a specified time in the future.[6] In socially determined contractual organizations, part of this agreement—and hence part of the behavior—involves work. Unlike familial and political forms, contractual organizations are thus potentially almost infinitely flexible, being limited in principle only by the kinds of agreements people in a culture can make. Not only can their size vary, but through the device of contract itself, external social content of organizational roles can potentially be limited. Contractual organizations can therefore be "more or less" socially determined, and if less, can be relatively free to adapt physically to technology. An important explicit purpose of a contract can, under certain conditions, actually be the prevention or control of the social determination of organization structure. Thus, a contract is also a major basis of both technologically determined and pluralistic work organization as well. The crucial difference between such contractual forms and those that are socially determined is that in the latter, the contractual agreement entails a multiplicity of activities, only some of which are work-connected. Participation in work thus involves introducing other activities into the work situation, just as it does with other socially determined work organizations.

Contractual organizations range from situations in which an employer simply hires people to work for him in essentially the same way as is common in our own culture, to situations where people join together for a variety of social and ceremonial functions, including work, on some mutually understood basis. Contractual mutual aid societies entailing obligations to work are, for example, very common. Contractual work organizations can also take the form of ascriptively constituted groups, such as an age-grade society or a guild, engaged as a whole to perform work. The Dahomean *dokpwe* would be a case in point. It consists for the most part of young men who cooperate in bride-work, but is expandable to include others as well. It performs a variety of ceremonial functions, in addition to hiring itself out for work.[7] Eighty-six contractual organizations appear in our sample.

Mixed cases. We therefore conclude that it makes sense to speak con-

[6] Kingsley Davis, *Human Society* (New York: The Macmillan Company, 1949), p. 470.
[7] Melville J. Herskovits, *Dahomey* (New York: J. J. Augustin, 1937), pp. 63-77.

cretely of familial, political, and contractual types of socially determined work organizations. At first thought it might appear that the possibility of mixed cases would present problems. Two kinds of apparently mixed cases are evident. In the first type, two, or conceivably all three, principles of social recruitment operate simultaneously. On this score, several instances of apparently combined political and familial, as well as political and contractual, recruitment were found; other conceivable simultaneous combinations did not occur. On closer examination all of these instances proved actually to be political, in that the political element was so thoroughly dominant that the presence of the other criteria had no discernible effect. Examples would be the forced political recruitment of several families as groups, or the conclusion of a "contract" under severe duress. The second type of mixed case, in which different parts of the same organization are recruited in different ways, proved to be of greater interest. Forty-eight such cases occurred, all involving families working together with extra workers hired by the family on some contractual basis. After initially analyzing this situation as a fourth, separate type, it was found that these organizations did not differ significantly in their effects from contractual forms. They were thus classified accordingly, though it will occasionally prove expedient, particularly in the next chapter, to treat them as a special subtype of contractual organization. It is significant that this type turned out to be contractual rather than familial; apparently, the presence of contractual principles in any part of a work organization lends a contractual cast to the entire structure.

Social base and development. It is thus the case that all socially determined work organizations, in contrast to production determined forms, have a readily identifiable, concrete social base. Furthermore, as Table 2.4 shows, the prevailing type of social base is related to the state of social development. The distribution shown is, in general, about what one would expect theoretically, and of course it reflects the decline of pro-

Table 2.4

Type of Society and Subtype of Work Organization

Type of society	Production determined	Familial	Political	Contractual
I and II	46	5	1	7
III	28	41	14	31
IV	22	27	33	21
V	0	16	35	27

Subtype of Organization

duction determined in favor of socially determined forms. Familial work organization is, along with the human family, ubiquitous. It receives its greatest relative impetus with the advent of sedentary agriculture in a context of exclusive proprietorship enjoyed by kinship groups, and later declines in favor of political and contractual forms. Specialized political units, on the other hand, require some minimal degree of institutional elaboration and begin to be significantly reflected in organized work only with the advent of sedentary agriculture. As might readily be expected, they receive their greatest impetus with centralized government when, in accordance with the theory outlined earlier, they begin relatively to displace familial forms as political units gain increasing control over resources.

Contractual work organization presents an interesting and somewhat different picture. As with political organization, its extensive application to work depends on some degree of institutional elaboration. Unlike political organization, however, it is not necessarily directly implicated in patterns of proprietary control over land, and thus appears in varied forms over our entire sample, except under highly primitive conditions. With the advent of centralized government and the consequent tendency for political organization to monopolize all forms of work, contractual organization appears to suffer somewhat. Curiously enough, the advent of complex stratification seems to entail a reversal of this trend and a relative upswing in the incidence of contractual work organization along with political forms. This development—which we shall explain later—combined with the demise of production determined work and the decline of familial forms, sets the stage for political and contractual forms as the two major "competing" ways of organizing work on the eve of industrialization. This competition is of course retained to some extent in modern industrial society.

The crucial question remains of whether differences in the social base of socially determined work organizations have any effect on their performance characteristics. Our model predicts that in the case of production determined organization, variations in social base would not have any such effect, and we shall find that indeed they do not. However, in the case of socially determined forms, our model predicts that type of social base would have implications for performance, because the characteristics of the social unit forming the base are presumably infused into the structure of the work organization, thereby affecting its operations. We shall find that this prediction is borne out by our data, and in ways consistent with other theoretical considerations. Relevant findings are presented in the next section. It proved expedient to present them along with our findings concerning over-all differences in performance of production determined, as opposed to all socially determined, forms. We thus now turn to a consideration of both of these questions.

PERFORMANCE CHARACTERISTICS

Our main emphasis here will be on efficiency, rather than effectiveness or innovative capacity, because of the nature of available data. Our findings concerning efficiency will, however, permit us to make certain inferences about probable effectiveness and innovative capacity. We shall focus on three aspects of organization: *manpower allocation, authority structure,* and *rationality.* The choice of these aspects for study was governed both by theoretical and by practical considerations. Manpower allocation, authority structure, and rationality are among the most important dimensions of complex organization, and also represent areas in which data permitting at least rough measures of efficiency were available for substantial numbers of organizations in our sample. Our strategy will be to construct a model describing a "perfectly efficient" work organization in each of these three areas, and then to measure differences in degree of deviation from this model by both organizational type and type of society.

Manpower Allocation

Manpower allocation is the pattern of distribution of people to the work organization during the course of its operation. In this regard, work organizations may be *temporary* or *permanent,* depending on whether they exist some of the time or all of the time, respectively. Permanent organizations may further be classed as *variable* or *constant* in size, depending on whether they add and subtract members periodically, or do not, respectively. Successful production demands that manpower allocation be at least adequate to the *work load* (the amount of human energy required to carry on the technology). As to work load, technologies are *intermittent,* if they require work only some of the time, or *continuous,* if they require at least some work all of the time. Continuous technologies may be either *variable* or *constant* as to work load, depending respectively on whether their human energy requirements fluctuate or remain the same during the course of the process.

A moment's reflection will show that "perfect efficiency" in manpower allocation is possible (though certainly by no means guaranteed) only where intermittent work is carried on by temporary organizations, continuous variable work by permanent variable organizations, and continuous constant work by permanent constant organizations. It is physically impossible for temporary organizations to carry on sustained, continuous work. All other combinations are perfectly possible physically, in the sense that the work can be performed effectively. They are, however, all inefficient as to manpower allocation in that they inevitably at some point in the process result in more people being present than are minimally necessary to do the work. A permanent organization of constant size will, for example, remain constant in size over the fluctuations in work load of any continuous variable technology it may be carrying on; it will thus provide adequate manpower for peak loads, but "too much" manpower during slack periods.

Work load, manpower allocation, and efficiency. Table 2.5 shows the actual relationship of manpower allocation to work load in our sample

Table 2.5

Work Load and Manpower Allocation

Type of work load	Manpower allocation		
	Temporary	Permanent and variable	Permanent and constant
Intermittent	74 *	42	63
Continuous and variable	0	88 *	58
Continuous and constant	1	10	19 *

* *Efficient, or potentially efficient, manpower allocation.*

of organizations. About half the organizations prove to be "efficient" in manpower allocation (that is, potentially so), while the remaining half are structured in such a way that they would have to be inefficient. From our basic model we would expect production determined organizations to be more efficient than socially determined organizations; on the basis of our discussion in the preceding section we would expect, among socially determined organizations, contractual forms to be the most efficient, and political organizations the least. Table 2.6 shows that these expectations are borne out, except that familial organizations appear to be at least as efficient in manpower allocation as are contractual forms, if not a bit more so. This exception is probably due to the relatively restricted scale of familial work, which perhaps allows familial organizations to remain somewhat immune from the influences of various development processes. For the same reason, this exception is not very important, in-

Table 2.6

Type of Work Organization and Efficiency of Manpower Allocation

Type of work organization	Manpower allocation	
	Efficient	Inefficient
Production determined	79	17
Familial	49	40
Political	14	69
Contractual	39	37

asmuch as this type of work declines with development and is thus of relatively less significance for later industrial organization than are larger scale operations. What is important here is that production determined organization is the most efficient type, political organization the least, and that contractual forms are considerably more efficient than are political forms.

Social development and efficiency of manpower allocation. Given this finding, along with the previously demonstrated effect of preindustrial social development on the relative incidence of various types of work organization, we would expect social development to produce a trend toward increasingly less efficient manpower allocation. As Table 2.7 in-

Table 2.7

Type of Society and Efficiency of Manpower Allocation

Type of society	Manpower allocation	
	Efficient	Inefficient
I and II	37	22
III	59	55
IV	48	55
V	37	41

dicates, this is basically what happens. However, this trend is much less marked than our theory might suggest. Furthermore, when one moves from society type IV to society type V—just at the point where the complete loss of production determined organizations would supposedly produce a truly great increase in inefficiency—the trend toward inefficiency seems to level off, and possibly even reverse itself slightly. This effect can only partly be explained by the fact that the incidence of contractual organizations, which are relatively likely to be efficient, increases at this point. As Table 2.8 shows, it appears that social development itself has

Table 2.8

Type of Society and Percent Efficient Manpower Allocation
by Type of Organization

Percent with efficient manpower allocation

Type of society	Production determined	Familial	Political	Contractual
I and II	83	0	0	17
III	90	50	17	39
IV	82	63	6	52
V	*	75	35	56

* No production determined organizations appear in society type V.

an independent, positive, direct effect on efficiency of manpower allocation quite apart from the over-all but indirect effect just described. For each separate type of socially determined work organization, the greater the degree of preindustrial social development, the more efficient the allocation of manpower, particularly in the case of contractual forms. It is important to notice that a similar effect is not present for production determined organization. The actual over-all decrease in efficiency shown in Table 2.7 is thus due solely to the fact that social development results in a shift to increasingly inefficient *types* of work organization. Until the advent of complex stratification, the negative effect of the shift away from production determined to political forms outweighs the direct positive effect. With the advent of complex stratification, however, the positive effect begins to outweigh the negative one. We shall explore the reasons for this apparent change in the next chapter. Suffice it to say for the present that under certain conditions contractual organizations, and to a lesser extent political ones, become involved in developmental processes of their own, which offer clues to the ultimate transformation to industrially appropriate forms of organized work.

Potential industrial effectiveness. Although it proved difficult to develop any direct measures of effectiveness of the organizations in our sample relative to industrial production (to do so would require the observation of direct attempts to employ these organizations in industrial work), such indirect estimates as could be developed suggest that the picture may not be quite so bleak as our model suggests. We have already seen that socially determined forms are more likely to be permanent than are production determined forms. It also appears that preindustrial social development brings increasingly continuous types of technology, and in this respect too moves work closer to the industrial norm, as Table 2.9

Table 2.9

Type of Society and Work Load

| Type of society | Work load | | |
	Intermittent	Continuous variable	Continuous constant
I and II	54	3	3
III	64	44	7
IV	50	44	11
V	15	55	9

shows. Inasmuch as the technology of sedentary agriculture is likely to be more continuous than that of gathering, hunting, or fishing, we would expect such a shift to occur. Most traditional continuous work, being mostly agricultural, is of the variable work load variety (for example, peak loads during planting and harvesting). With further social development we would expect a broader societal division of labor combined with an exchange system to permit some equalization of work load, with another relative shift to continuous constant technology; this shift, as Table 2.9 indicates, is present but rather weak.

However, we should not be too encouraged by these findings. They seem to derive largely from certain peculiarities of agriculture as such. Furthermore, relatively little continuous constant work emerges. The problem of the adaptation of socially determined forms to technologies requiring a really complex division of labor still remains moot, as well. In our sample, the maximum number of differentiated activities found for any one organization was 12, certainly far less than is found in any complex industrial process. There is also considerable presumptive evidence that social determination cannot readily yield a division of labor of much greater complexity. We conclude, therefore, that the data on manpower allocation confirm our hypothesis that preindustrial social development generates tendencies toward increasing inefficiency in organized work not only because of the shift it engenders from production determined to socially determined forms, but because it continues to produce shifts toward increasingly inefficient socially determined forms. We have discovered some exceptions to this trend, but they provide more clues to possible ways in which this trend might be reversed than actual contrary evidence.

Authority Structure

Let us now examine another, quite different, measure of efficiency. If our theory is correct, this measure would be expected to yield essentially parallel results. It is based on authority structure, under the assumption that some organizations have a more complicated authority structure than is technologically necessary to perform their work. Such a supposition is certainly a rather popular one and is often encountered in the literature as well.[8]

A work organization consists not only of a collection of people, but also a system of *roles* that these people, in their capacities as members of the work organization, are expected to play vis-à-vis one another. Organizational roles not only involve distinctive activities, but also entail expectations about how people playing any given role are to relate to people playing other given roles. One very important aspect of such expectations is authority. *Authority* is defined as *institutionalized power:* that is, the expected ability of one person to control the activities of another person or other persons, by virtue of his and their given organizational roles. The *authority structure* of a work organization is thus the pattern exhibited by its roles when they are ordered according to the amounts of authority they convey in relation to one another. Any two roles that do not convey differential authority, either directly or indirectly, will be said to occupy the same *level of authority*. All work organizations thus entail one or more levels of authority.

Determinants of authority structure. What determines the number of levels of authority in any work organization? In the case of socially determined organizations the answer is presumably simple. The number of levels of authority in any socially determined work organization is set by the number of hierarchical status levels in the external social unit from which the work organization derives; the structure of the former is merely reflected in the structure of the latter. With production determined work organizations, however, the answer is less simple. Broadly speaking,

[8] See, for example, Michel Crozier, *The Bureaucratic Phenomenon,* trans. by the author (Chicago: University of Chicago Press, 1964); Robert Presthus, *The Organizational Society* (New York: Alfred A. Knopf, Inc., 1962).

since organization structure here presumably results from planning relative to technological requirements, we would expect the number of levels of authority to be determined solely by some aspect of the technology. According to "classical" organization theory, the major planned technological function of authority is the coordination of differentiated activities. Let us assume for purposes of argument that coordination is the only function of authority and that authority is the sole means of such coordination (assumptions not too unrealistic where work is not mechanized). Let us also assume an upper limit on the number of different activities that any one person can reliably coordinate. It then follows that in any production determined work organization, the number of authority levels will be determined precisely by the number of differentiated activities in the technology, allowing for some margin of ignorance and error in planning and adaptation. Furthermore, it follows from this same argument that in work organizations of *all* types, the number of differentiated activities in the technology sets a lower limit on the number of levels of authority consistent with effective over-all work performance, whether the authority structure is planned relative to technology or not.

The foregoing model permits us to make an argument with respect to authority structure parallel to the argument made with respect to manpower allocation. We would expect production determined organizations to possess the exact number of authority levels predicted from the technology. By dint of "natural selection" we would similarly expect any persisting socially determined organizations to possess at least the same number of authority levels. However, because the authority structure of socially determined forms is determined independently of technological considerations, we would expect a significant number of these organizations to possess *more* levels of authority than technologically necessary, and hence in this respect to be inefficient. There is no reason to suppose that such organizations could not perform work effectively, but in the process of doing so they would simply devote more time, energy, and personnel to the exercise of authority than would be required on purely technological grounds.

In order to test this hypothesis we must first establish the exact relationship we would expect between degree of technological differentiation and number of authority levels on purely technological grounds, in the absence of social considerations. This relationship is governed by the maximum number of different activities that can be reliably coordinated by any one person. "*Any* one person" is an important phrase, because people undoubtedly differ in their ability to coordinate activities. Organizations, however, must be structured in such a way that anyone eligible for a particular role will be able to perform it, at least minimally. Consequently, we would not expect the unquestioned fact of individual differences to have any essential effect on our model.

Previous research by this author suggests that the maximum number of differentiated activities that *anyone* can be expected to coordinate in a reliably persisting work organization is four.[9] In light of this finding and our earlier assumptions, we would therefore expect the following: (1) wholly undifferentiated technologies would require only one level of authority; (2) technologies involving from 2 through 4 differentiated activities would require two levels of authority; (3) technologies involving from 5 through 16 differentiated activities would require three levels of authority, and so forth. Sufficient data were available on 88 cases in the sample to fit them to this model. For each of these cases, the degree of technological differentiation was determined by counting the maximum number of different activities ever performed simultaneously during the course of the work, adding to this figure the total number of sets of such activities differentiated serially, and finally adding one extra activity if any activity ever required the combined effort of several persons working in unison. The resulting figure ranged from 1 through 12 over the sample. Similarly, for each case, the number of levels of authority—ranging from 1 through 6 in the sample—was reconstructed from the ethnographic description.

Technological differentiation, authority, and efficiency. The relationship between technological differentiation and authority structure is shown in Table 2.10 and is consistent with our model, except for 7 instances of "too few" authority levels. In 4 of these cases the assumption that all

Table 2.10

Technological Differentiation and Number of Authority Levels

Number of levels of authority

Technolgical differentiation	Under 3	3	Over 3
Fewer than 5 activities	51	1 *	0
5 or more activities	7	19	10 *

* All 11 "excessive" cases are socially determined.

[9] Stanley H. Udy, Jr., *Organization of Work* (New Haven: HRAF Press, 1959), pp. 78-88.

coordination occurs through authority was clearly not met; the other 3 cases are unexplained. As anticipated, in several (11) cases, more authority levels appear than are technologically required. According to our theory, all of these cases should be socially determined. As Table 2.11 shows, all of them indeed are.

Table 2.11

Type of Work Organization and Efficiency of Authority Structure

| | Authority structure | |
Type of organization	Efficient	Inefficient
Production determined	35	0
Familial	20	5
Political	9	4
Contractual	13	2

Though frequencies are low, Table 2.11 also suggests that political organizations are less efficient than are familial or contractual forms in authority structure, just as is the case with manpower allocation. One presumes that this is so because political institutions generally are apt to involve more ramified hierarchies than are other social structures and are consequently especially prone to multiplication of internal authority differences.

Social development and efficiency of authority structure. These various trends, when combined with the effect of social development on type of work system, suggest that the implications of social development for efficiency of authority structure are similar to the implications for efficiency of manpower allocation; namely, social development results in increasingly less efficient forms of organized work. Table 2.12 is consistent with this hypothesis, though frequencies are again low.

Table 2.12 suggests another possible parallel with manpower allocation. Again, it appears that between society types IV and V there may be a reversal of the trend toward inefficiency. Though frequencies are too small for a conclusive analysis, this reversal as it appears in the data is due solely to the fact that 7 of the 15 contractual organizations reported appear in society types IV and V—2 in IV and 5 in V—and all are efficient in authority structure. (Two of the 8 other contractual forms

Table 2.12

*Type of Society and Efficiency of
Authority Structure*

	Authority structure	
Type of society	Efficient	Inefficient
I and II	21	0
III	34	4
IV	13	5
V	8	2

are inefficient, and appear elsewhere.) In contrast, neither familial nor political organizations seem to grow any more efficient in authority structure with social development; if anything, they appear to become less so. The independent direct reverse effect of social development on efficiency thus seems to occur here too, but is less marked, and may be confined only to contractual forms.

Our findings with respect to authority structure thus parallel and strengthen our findings with respect to manpower allocation. Because of the changes it engenders in prevailing type of work organization, traditional social development involves strong pressures toward decreased efficiency in organized work. With the advent of complex stratification, however, these pressures seem to be offset somewhat by apparently direct counterpressures toward increased efficiency. Contractual organization evidently plays an important part in this development.

Role Content and Rationality

We shall now examine a third measure of efficiency, again to ascertain whether parallel findings emerge. Since all organized work is carried on in a social setting, it is inevitable that the substantive content of roles in any work organization will include some elements other than work activity. Non-work elements in work roles have the potential, at least, of interfering with efficiency by taking time and attention away from work itself.

The problem of attention. This argument, however, must be modified by one important consideration. Non-work elements in work roles lead to inefficiency only to the extent that the technology involved requires undivided attention. Where it does not, non-work elements make no direct technical difference. Technology requires undivided attention to the degree that it entails tasks that have to be performed rapidly under pressure. Such a circumstance is most likely to exist where various unpredictable events occur during a process having highly interdependent activities, and thus require constant attention to adaptation and adjustment, usually through preplanned complex programs of alternative courses of action with decision rules. There was no precise way to measure the extent of undivided attention required by any technology. However, we could make some simple "yes-no" judgments in answer to the question of whether undivided attention seemed essential to the success of the work. With agriculture, the answer was usually "no": under most (but not all) climatic conditions, pressure of time does not demand immediate response to adaptive problems. Large-scale hunting, in contrast, very often did seem to require undivided attention, particularly if a herd was surrounded and constantly moving about.[10]

Social development and attention. Applying this crude distinction, we thus observe that traditional social development involves a trend away from work requiring undivided attention, as Table 2.13 shows. Much

Table 2.13

Social Development and Required Undivided Attention to Work

	Undivided attention required	
Type of society	Yes	No
I and II	21	22
III	24	61
IV	21	55
V	7	62

(though not all) of this trend is due to a shift away from hunting and fishing in food production in favor of agriculture. Social development may thus result in a decline in inefficiency. However, this decline may be a consequence of a "fool's paradise" effect—there is simply less *opportunity* for organizations to be inefficient as a result of extensive role content. What is really important is the decline in technological stimulus that might evoke attention to problems of efficiency on this score.

Adaptive capacity, rationality, and organizational type. A more critical question is that of the capacity of work organizations to adapt to situations requiring undivided attention to work. Two considerations are

[10] Ibid., pp. 16-17.

fundamentally relevant here. The first is the basic type of work organization. Because of their relative freedom from external social demands, we would expect production determined organizations to be more adaptable than socially determined organizations to work requiring undivided attention, other things being equal. A second consideration is the presence or absence of administrative rationality. The structure of any organization will be called *rational* to the extent that it involves administrative devices to limit the content of work roles to the work itself. Three such devices are important for present purposes: *specific job assignment* (explicit assignment of particular persons to particular work roles); *compensatory rewards* (allocation of money and/or goods in kind in return for participation); and *performance emphasis* (dependence of the quantity of the reward on the quantity and/or quality of work done).[11] If at least two of these devices were present, the organization concerned was classified as *administratively rational;* others were deemed *not administratively rational.*

As previously indicated, rationality is irrelevant to performance unless the work requires undivided attention. Under such circumstances, too, rationality may be relatively irrelevant to production determined work, which is by its very nature already segmented from social structure generally, and thus presumably requires no administrative devices to segment it further. For socially determined organizations performing work requiring undivided attention, however, the presence of administrative rationality would be highly critical, if not crucial, to efficient performance. The question then is: under conditions of work requiring undivided attention, which forms of organized work are most likely to be rationally organized? If efficiency is to be maintained, socially determined organizations in particular would have to be so. As Table 2.14 shows, this indeed seems to be the case with contractual organizations. Apparently, as might be anticipated, contractual agreements often seem to limit the social content of work roles. Political organizations, where diffuse political obligations tend to be carried over into the work situation without administrative restriction, do so less. Surprisingly, production determined forms are just as likely to be rationally organized as are contractual forms. This may be because they are merely responsive to the attention requirements of the technology in conformance with our model; rationality will enhance performance even if very few social elements are present. Another possible explanation derives from the findings of a previous study, which suggested that for highly segmented organizations rational characteristics have the added function of institutionalizing motivation in the absence

[11] Stanley H. Udy, Jr., "'Bureaucracy' and 'Rationality' in Weber's Organization Theory," *American Sociological Review*, 24 (1959), 791-95.

Table 2.14

**Type of Organization and Administrative Rationality
with Undivided Attention Required**

Administrative rationality

Type of organization	Present	Absent
Production determined	38	10
Familial *	0	0
Political	4	12
Contractual	8	2

** In no familial organization for which we had
relevant data was undivided attention required.*

of—rather than as an offset to—social content.[12] Viable production determined organizations would thus tend to possess rational characteristics for reasons in addition to those suggested by the present model.

The low frequencies in Table 2.14 reflect the decline, with social development, of work requiring undivided attention. Socially determined organizations thus have relatively few opportunities to be inefficient on this score in the first place. No familial organizations were found to be carrying on this type of work.

Determinants of rationality. The question still remains as to why some work organizations are rationally structured whereas others are not. In the case of socially determined work organizations, our basic model would lead us to suppose that rational organization arises for purely external social reasons and never as a response to technological requirements. Any efficiency resulting from rationality would thus be wholly fortuitous. In the case of production determined work organizations, we are confronted with two competing theories: first, that rationality results from planned adaptation to technology; and second, that although it is not directly caused by external social forces, it results from them through a process of natural selection. Table 2.15, alone and in conjunction with Table 2.14, presents data relevant to a test of these various hypotheses.

Table 2.15 shows the differential tendency of the various types of work organization to be rational in the absence of any technological necessity for them to be so. Production determined, and—most notably—contractual organizations have marked tendencies toward rationality even under

[12] Stanley H. Udy, Jr., "Administrative Rationality, Social Setting, and Organizational Development," *American Journal of Sociology,* 68 (1962), 299-308.

Table 2.15

Type of Organization and Administrative Rationality with Undivided Attention Not Required

Administrative rationality

Type of organization	Present	Absent
Production determined	9	11
Familial	6	70
Political	0	47
Contractual	34	23

such circumstances. A comparison of Tables 2.14 and 2.15 suggests that production determined organizations are somewhat more likely to be rational as a result of planned adaptation than as a result of natural selection, though both mechanisms appear to be operative. Contractual organizations seem to behave largely as our model predicts; apparently they are basically institutionalized in such a way that they are quite likely to be rational, regardless of technological considerations. However, a comparison of the two tables suggests that contractual organizations may be somewhat responsive to technological requirements, despite their socially determined character. So may political organizations, apparently, but not very frequently.

The over-all result of these various trends is that traditional social development results not only in less attention being paid to efficiency of organizational role content, because fewer occasions arise for such attention, but also in a decrease in the capacity of organizations to generate efficient role content even when it is technologically required, essentially because of a trend toward forms of organization less likely to be rational. Table 2.16 shows this over-all decrease, and also presents a breakdown by type of work organization, which is of considerable interest. From the table it appears that social development exerts an independent effect on rationality, just as it does on efficiency of manpower allocation, and possibly on efficiency of authority structure. In the case of rationality, however, the direction of this effect seems to differ by organizational type. Social development apparently results independently in *decreased* rationality for production determined and political forms and *increased* rationality for familial and contractual forms. Particularly significant for our purposes are its contrasting effects on political and contractual forms; contractual forms appear to retain, and even possibly increase, their

Table 2.16

Type of Society and Percentage of Work Organizations with Rational Administration by Type of Organization

Percent having rational administration

Type of society	Production determined	Familial	Political	Contractual	Total
I and II	70	0	*	*	62
III	79	0	22	60	36
IV and V	56	17	4	68	30

* No organizations reported in available data.

degree of rational organization, whereas political forms go in the opposite direction.

CONCLUSIONS

Our hypothesis that the course of preindustrial social development militates against the development of forms of work organization progressively more suited to industrial production is, in view of these findings, essentially confirmed, although the picture is more complex than our initial formulation would perhaps suggest. On the positive side, preindustrial social development does bring increasing continuity of work and more permanence in work organization. Both of these characteristics are presumably essential typical features of industrial work situations, and in a very real sense it may be said that traditional work, if it "progresses" at all, progresses toward these characteristics.

On the negative side, such developments are not secured without considerable cost to the efficiency and over-all effectiveness of organized work, relative to industrial requirements. Preindustrial social development generates a shift from production determined work organization to various forms of socially determined work organization, all of which are in general less efficient—based on measures relating to manpower allocation, authority structure, and role content—than are production determined forms. Politically based socially determined organizations are especially inefficient, and as development proceeds, the trend toward this particular form is accelerated. There is thus a tendency for organized work in traditional society to become bogged down in a morass of excess manpower, overly elaborate authority systems, and socially complex role requirements that tend to detract from work performance per se. To make matters worse, there is also a trend away from work situations that would tend to attract attention to the importance of rational role content in the first place.

Nevertheless, a certain amount of hope is mixed with these problems. In the first place, at later stages of social development socially determined forms of work organization tend to become somewhat more efficient, though they never achieve the efficiency of production determined organizations. This is especially true of contractual forms, which also appear, again in the later stages of preindustrial social development, to become relatively more numerous. It appears, therefore, that something tends to enhance the efficiency of socially determined work organization, and that the key to this development lies in contractual forms of work. In the second place, the over-all trend toward inefficiency, decreasing rationality, and unsuitability to industrial technology seems to result not from any direct effect of development on the work process itself, but rather from the effect of development on the type of work organization that prevails. Social development per se does not cause inefficiency, but it results in relatively inefficient forms of organized work. If different, more efficient, forms of work organization could somehow be instituted, they would thus presumably retain their inherent efficiencies regardless of the social setting.

We conclude, therefore, that it is possible: (1) that changes can occur in social structure generally that may render socially determined work as a whole less inefficient than we have generally found it to be; (2) that the development of contractual organizations is critical in this process; and (3) that changes in over-all type of work organization may alter the picture entirely. Such possibilities would seem to be very important in the development of viable industrial work processes, a topic to which we now turn.

Behavioral scientists have on the whole found it much easier to suggest reasons why industrial development is difficult or impossible than to explain how it occurs. This rather negativist proclivity has not been entirely without merit. Traditional society does present some very real barriers to industrialization, some of which we have just seen, and these barriers have not always been well recognized. Nevertheless, industrial development does take place, and it has sometimes occurred despite the dire predictions of pessimistic behavioral scientists. On the whole, the adoption of an industrial way of life, though it does involve problems, is apparently less difficult for traditional peoples than many anthropologists and sociologists had at one time supposed. From a human point of view this is doubtless a happy discovery, but it has often placed the behavioral scientist in the uncomfortable position of the physician whose theories have been disproved by the failure of the patient to die. He is personally pleased yet embarrassed because he cannot help being intellectually dissatisfied, particularly because many behavioral prognoses of disaster have seemingly rested on facts about which there was little disagreement. On the level of work organization, for example, our finding that organized work in newly developing areas is apt to be ineffective and inefficient by modern

CHAPTER THREE

The Transition to Industrial Work

industrial standards is corroborated by numerous accounts and reports. The International Labour Office tells us, for instance, that

In a tobacco factory in Uganda the management estimated that in the factory generally three Africans are required to produce what two Europeans can produce in Europe; in short, it takes more Africans than Europeans to handle a given machine output. . . . In a textile factory in the Belgian Congo where African women are employed in one machine operation, one worker operates two machines, while in Belgium one European woman operates four of the same machines. . . . In Ubangi-Chari the output of Africans on various forms of masonry work was only one-third to one-fourth that of workers in France performing the same type of operation.[1]

The same report also informs us that "the high rate of labour turnover has long been recognized as the most persistent feature of the African scene," and that "absenteeism is a serious labour problem in all African countries."[2] The literature provides similar examples from many areas of the world. There is thus little disagreement about the facts, or about the contention that successful industrialization requires some change in this and similar states of affairs.

INTERPRETATIONS

The problem, rather, has been one of interpreting the facts. The kinds of explanations that behavioral scientists have usually adduced to account for such conditions have drawn attention to factors making for their persistence, rather than mechanisms that might result in their change. Certain rather basic theoretical issues actually lie at the root of the matter. Sociologists characteristically employ two general modes of explanation in seeking to account for any social phenomenon. The first is cultural and psychologistic. It asserts that people behave as they do because they have learned certain cultural values and norms through the process of socialization. Triggered by exposure to some situation, people play roles prescribed by these values and norms. Social behavior thus, in effect, becomes a "theatrical" enterprise, and it can be analyzed and explained by studying either cultural content, personal attitudes, or some combination of the two. The second mode of explanation is ecological and structural. It assumes that people are motivated in basically similar ways, and asserts that differences in their behavior can therefore be explained by

[1] International Labour Office, *African Labour Survey*, Studies and Reports, New Series, No. 48 (Geneva: International Labour Office, 1958), 144-46.
[2] Ibid., pp. 144-46.

structural differences in the situations to which they are responding. Social behavior can thus be analyzed as a residue of what is allowable after structural impossibilities have been eliminated.

However, neither explanation is complete in and of itself. Neither can "explain" anything without at least implicitly assuming something about the other. Each therefore begs questions that the other presumably answers. Cultural-psychological explanations necessarily assume something about the structure of the situation to which the people are presumed to be responding. Ecological-structural explanations similarly assume some motivational state that presumably has been induced through the socialization process. Human behavior thus always results from some combination of psychological and ecological mechanisms. In a way, it is always a fusion of wants and possibilities. Efforts to proceed by only one of these explanations are apt to be misleading. In particular, they are likely to ignore some very potent sources of change inherent in the situation, which arise from a lack of congruence between the resultants of the two mechanisms represented. Man is both a cultural and a problem-solving animal; he responds both to what he already knows and feels, and to the exigencies of the immediate situation confronting him. It is the tension between these two sources of behavior that produces novel directions in his action. A purely cultural explanation of social behavior results in its being viewed simply as repetitive play-acting; a purely structural explanation similarly results in its being viewed simply as repetitive adaptation and adjustment. Neither explanation alone offers room for innovation and change.[3]

Cultural-psychologistic Theories

Herein lies the problem of much behavioral science theory of economic and industrial development. It is weighted toward persistence because it has been essentially one-sided. The emphasis has usually been cultural and psychologistic. Traditional culture is portrayed as involving certain normative patterns, which, when internalized through socialization, yield personality types totally unsuited to the economic and technical demands of modern industrial society. Thus McClelland stresses the importance for industrialization of the presence of a "need for achievement," and Hagen, the indispensability of values conducive to the development of innovative, entrepreneurial personalities. The relative absence of such "needs" and values in traditional societies therefore presents difficulties. Various neo-Weberian formulations similarly emphasize the

---

[3] For a more detailed discussion of this issue see the author's "Social Structural Analysis," *International Encyclopedia of the Social Sciences* (1968), XIV, 489-95.

problem of the lack of the "rational spirit" in traditional settings. By way of extension, some commentators phrase the situation in terms of the Parsons pattern variables: traditional culture is characterized generally by norms of diffuseness, particularism, affectivity, and ascription, whereas modern industrial culture leans heavily toward norms of specificity, universalism, neutrality, and performance.[4]

Without necessarily disputing the immediate descriptive accuracy of such characterizations, one may observe that a reliance on almost solely cultural-psychologistic mechanisms has two consequences. First, to the extent that it ignores the possibility of shifting structural exigencies, it leads to the impression that traditional society is homogeneous, stable, and characterized by massive inertia. Though not suggesting that change is impossible altogether, it implies that change is very difficult, because it can come about only through a shift in cultural values and via the socialization process. Second, this approach suggests that people are much more inflexible in responding to immediate situational exigencies than they actually appear to be; it emphasizes the acting out of roles, rather than the solving of problems. Thus it leads to the view, for example, that rational administrative behavior and widespread efficiency in work are confined to modern industrial society, on the grounds that only in modern culture are norms of rationality and efficiency broadly institutionalized. The implication is that people in preindustrial settings cannot behave rationally and efficiently in work situations, simply because they have not been brought up that way.

One can hardly deny that social change *can* come about through shifts in cultural values. Unquestionably, also, rationality and efficiency in work are more likely to be realized if they are supported by general internalized values. It is also probably the case that such values, as general institutions, are largely confined to modern industrial culture. However, it does not follow from these considerations that traditional society is essentially unchanging, or that rationality and efficiency in organization are confined to modern industrial experience. The data presented in the preceding chapter indeed show that traditional society is far from unchanging, and its variations have profound implications for organized work. Furthermore, our findings have clearly indicated that the contention that rationality and efficiency in organized work is wholly an indus-

---

[4] David C. McClelland, *The Achieving Society* (Princeton, N.J.: D. Van Nostrand Co., Inc., 1961); Everett E. Hagen, *On the Theory of Social Change* (Homewood, Ill.: Dorsey Press, 1962); Bert F. Hoselitz, *Sociological Aspects of Economic Growth* (New York: The Free Press, 1960), pp. 28-42; Gino Germani, *Politica y Sociedad en una Epoca de Transicion* (Buenos Aires: Editorial Paidos, 1962), pp. 75-81. On the pattern variables themselves see Talcott Parsons, *et al.*, *Toward a General Theory of Action* (Cambridge, Mass.: Harvard University Press, 1951), pp. 80-88.

trial phenomenon is simply not true. Rationally organized efficiency in work is not at all uncommon in preindustrial experience, and in fact characterizes most of organized work in highly primitive settings. It is less likely to occur in more complex traditional societies, but is never completely unknown even there.

Of more importance for present purposes, however, are our findings as to how different forms of work organization, together with their performance characteristics, are produced. They only partly derive from internalized cultural values, and herein lies the basic reason why the structure of role expectations within a work organization can sometimes be quite at variance with both the general normative prescriptions of its cultural context and the over-all personal attitudes of its members.[5] The main causal sequence appears to be as follows. The general cultural and social context (including internalized cultural values) determines the way in which the structure of the work system is defined and perceived—specifically, what elements are to be adapted to which other elements, what problems are to be solved, and in particular how the work organization is to be related to the rest of the work system. The way the work system is structured, in turn, determines the form of the work organization, including its internal norms and role expectations, which, in turn, determines its performance characteristics. Thus, for a variety of general structural and cultural reasons, which we have already examined, work systems in highly primitive societies are defined as requiring the adaptation of organization to physical exigencies independently of the social setting. The result is a production determined work organization, with a high degree of rationality and performance efficiency. The reason does not lie in the personalities of its members, but rather in the fact that they define the problems they are trying to solve so as to exclude from their perception and consideration elements that would render their behavior nonrational and inefficient. Similarly, in more complex traditional societies, work systems are defined in such a way as to include broader social and cultural elements directly in the organization structure. The result is a socially determined work organization, which, because of these general social and cultural elements, entails "multiple interests" that militate against rationality and efficiency in work, if only because they compete with work for attention.[6] Again it is a question of the way

[5] For a discussion of the general case of this situation and its illustration in a different context see Peter M. Blau and W. Richard Scott, *Formal Organizations* (San Francisco: Chandler Publishing Company, 1962), pp. 100-108.

[6] See Robert Redfield, "The Folk Society," *American Journal of Sociology*, 42 (1947), 293-308; Manning Nash, *Primitive and Peasant Economic Systems* (San Francisco: Chandler Publishing Company, 1966), pp. 23-24.

the problems to be solved are defined, rather than one of personality characteristics.

The foregoing interpretation is supported further by an analysis of deviant cases. Production determined work organizations are, as we have seen, roughly equally rational and efficient in any society, including traditional ones (where, however, they would be unusual). Thus, if for whatever reason, a work organization in a highly traditional society is, contrary to the usual pattern, production determined, the resulting work will be rationally and efficiently conducted, despite the fact that socially determined organizations exhibiting quite the opposite internal normative and performance characteristics may be the prevailing forms in that same society. Similarly, socially determined work organizations still remain inefficient and lacking in rational structure when they (exceptionally) appear in relatively primitive settings. It is primarily the way in which the structure of the work system and the problems to be solved are defined and perceived that determines the organizational form and its performance characteristics, rather than internalized cultural values.

Thus the foregoing complex of mechanisms is largely responsible for the lack of rational organization and technical capacity, and for the presence of inefficiency, in organized work in newly industrializing societies. Nevertheless, we have also seen that general social and cultural contextual elements do exert a direct effect on performance under certain conditions. Under those conditions, a cultural-psychologistic interpretation may well be appropriate. Interestingly enough, however, this direct effect is not present in production determined organizations, presumably because their structure does not allow for the possibility of a direct contextual influence on performance. It appears only in socially determined organizations, in which the members of the organization are expected to adapt to general cultural and social influences as part of the problem. Insofar as industrialization is concerned, this effect, though small in comparison with the preceding one, is exactly the opposite to what is often alleged in cultural-psychologistic analyses of industrial development. It is in a *positive* direction: the more highly developed the traditional society, the more rational and efficient are the particular types of socially determined work organizations in it.

Insofar as the organization of work is concerned, newly industrializing societies therefore face one or both of two possibilities. First, socially determined forms of organized work may themselves become somewhat better adapted to industrial application. As development occurs, they do seem to tend toward more rational organization and somewhat greater technical efficiency. One of the reasons for this trend is, as we have seen, that they tend to adopt contractual forms. To some degree, though, the same trend is present in politically structured work organizations. However, as long as both of these forms remain socially determined, it would appear that the possibilities for enhanced efficiency and technical capacity are greatly limited. They would depend on a general change in the entire culture and social structure in the direction of strong norms of rationality and efficiency, which would be transmitted through the socialization process and thus emerge in all aspects of life, including work. As we have seen, one of the main problems with the cultural-psychologistic approach to industrial development has been the assumption that socialization is the only way in which modern forms of work organization can come into being. It is indeed possible, in principle, for organizational development to occur in this manner to at least some degree. However, in view of our discussion and findings up to this point, this path to development would at best be extremely difficult, with its eventual success highly improbable. It is no wonder that behavioral theories of economic development have often led to pessimistic prognostications; most have, in effect, assumed that industrial development depends organizationally on enhancing the efficiency and industrial adaptability of socially determined forms of work, and to do so beyond narrow limits is virtually impossible.

An Alternative Approach

Fortunately, however, industrial development need not be solely a battle for men's minds. A more promising course lies in the alteration of the way in which the structure of the work system is defined and perceived, with rationality, efficiency, and capacity for industrial effectiveness simply following from the ensuing shift in the form of work organization. The problem is thus one of discovering how socially determined forms of organized work become transformed into another type of structure better suited to industrial production. As we have seen, a return to production determined organization would appear to be out of the question in a newly industrializing society. However, technologically determined organization is a real possibility. Furthermore, technologically determined work allows for autonomy of organization, without at the same time requiring a unitary cultural goal structure in the setting. Pluralistic organization is another possibility. It too allows for a technological focus, as well as a choice of production objectives. Actually, certain external conditions bring forth a variety of adaptive responses in this direction in both socially determined work organization and its setting. These responses set mechanisms in motion that result in the development of technologically determined work, while at the same time enhancing the efficiency of remaining socially determined forms. Ultimately, and subsequently, pluralistic forms of organized work arise out of this state of affairs. This entire process is fraught with numerous pitfalls and dead ends and is neither evolutionary nor inevitable. Its successful completion depends on the presence of a variety of external conditions, at the right time.

The crucial intervening mechanism in this process is the development of contractual forms of work organization. No work organization can achieve a specifically technological focus unless it enjoys a considerable degree of autonomy vis-à-vis its social setting. Contractual organization is the only form of socially determined work offering this possibility. Familial and political forms are imbedded in diverse social obligations. Contractual forms, in contrast, focus on specific problems with which the parties involved are concerned. They therefore not only offer the possibility of relative disengagement from social structure, but may also even become technologically determined. This disengagement, in fact, lies at the basis of their greater rationality and efficiency relative to other types of socially determined work organization. It is thus through the growth of contractual organization and its interaction with various circumstances in the social setting, that the transition from socially to technologically determined forms of work is engendered.

THE DEVELOPMENT OF CONTRACTUAL WORK

To the inhabitant of modern industrial society, where contractual work is as commonplace as noncontractual work is rare, the picture presented by contractual work in traditional society is apt to be a bit mystifying. Contrary to what some have supposed, the weight of available evidence suggests that contractual socially determined work probably exists in some form in all traditional societies, but is never very widespread and is likely to play a definitely subordinate role to various alternative forms of work, which industrial man would regard as archaic. In short, contractual work seems initially to be indulged by traditional peoples only if there is no practical alternative to it. It emerges as something of a last-ditch response to a shortage of labor after familial and political modes of recruitment, together with their extensions and variants, have failed. When it does appear, it is very likely to be so thoroughly circumscribed by more dominant forms of work that it has little effect on future development.

Yet this picture is less gloomy than one might think, for such labor shortages are frequent. Familial organizations in particular suffer from intrinsic manpower limitations, since they are by nature restricted to a given network of kin relations. This situation poses routine problems in the face of heavy seasonal work loads in agriculture especially, and also in construction work to a lesser degree. As Table 3.1 shows, however, the response in our sample to a work load too heavy for the familial group

Table 3.1

Response of Familial Organization to Variable Work Loads

	Type of organization		
Work load	Familial only	Familial with reciprocity	Familial with contract
Constant	22	23	19
Variable	1	62	29

to handle alone is at least as likely to be an extension of the familial principle to reciprocity among families, as it is to be an effort to recruit workers by contractual means.

Reciprocity

Such reciprocity is of two general varieties. The first, the discrete type, characteristically occurs where extra work of a nonroutine nature is required by one family at a time, and simply involves "swaps" of equivalent time and manpower by pairs of families as the need arises. The second, the rotational type, is typically found applied when a need for extra work confronts many families at once, in a more or less routine way. It entails an often extensive pooled arrangement whereby several families work for one another in successive rotation. When the rotation cycle has been completed, all work obligations have been discharged. Both of these forms of reciprocity are extremely common, and they often exist side by side in the same society, with different names. Among the Bisayan Filipinos, for example, the discrete form is called a *palihog*. A common occasion for a *palihog* is house construction, though it occasionally appears in agriculture. The time and occasion for reciprocation are indefinite, but reciprocation is definitely expected, and in a situation requiring roughly equivalent amounts of time and effort. The same society also has a system of rotational reciprocity, called the *bolhon*, which is routinely used to work adjacent fields by neighbors during peak work periods in agriculture, such as field preparation, planting, and harvesting. One day is spent per plot, with the rotation running full cycle until everyone has done an equal amount of work for everyone else. If any member of the *bolhon* desires that more than a day's work be done for him, he is free to negotiate a contractual agreement with the other members to do extra work for pay.[7]

Similar paired systems of discrete and rotational reciprocity are rather widely reported elsewhere, as are specific linguistic terms designating them. The words for *palihog* and *bolhon* among the Maanyan, for instance, are *haweh* and *hando,* respectively; the medieval Saxon term for *bolhon* was *cyvar.*[8] Reciprocity, therefore, is well established as a solution to periodically heavy work loads in familial situations. Such arrangements, however, have the intrinsic difficulty of being incompatible with an unequal distribution of work to be done, since they almost universally rest on the expectation that all parties involved will ultimately perform equivalent amounts of work. They therefore tend to break down or be supplemented by other arrangements, in the face of unequal distributions of property. Such a situation potentially opens the door to contractual recruitment, with larger landholders simply hiring people to do extra work. The Bisayan system permits this, as we have seen. However, large landholders typically have access to political power and are thus likely to fill the breach with some form of forced political labor.

The typical tendency of organized work in a highly developed traditional society is thus toward familial organization supplemented by reciprocity among lower-class people with roughly equal holdings, combined with a superstructure of forced labor in varying forms and degrees politically imposed by larger landholders. In practice, as we shall see presently, this picture is apt to be somewhat moderated, but its essential features remain, and it is very difficult for contractual forms to achieve a significant breakthrough. Reciprocity suffices for low-level needs, and forced labor is cheaper than hired help.

Protocontractual Forms

Nevertheless, two varieties of protocontractual arrangements are fairly common under such circumstances and serve as a source of some moderation. Both are largely restricted to small landholders, and both are ordinarily tightly circumscribed by a dominant political work structure.

Employment of ascribed groups. The first case is an alternative to discrete reciprocity wherein some already constituted social group, such

[7] Donn V. Hart, "Barrio Caticugan," unpublished doctoral dissertation, Syracuse University, 1954, pp. 431-33.

[8] John H. Provinse, "Cooperative Ricefield Cultivation among the Siang Dyaks of Central Borneo," *American Anthropologist,* XXXIX (1937), 77-102; Frederic Seebohm, *The English Village Community,* 4th ed. (London: Longmans, Green and Co., Ltd., 1905), pp. 117-25.

as an age-grade association, hires itself out for work as a body to family proprietors on a discrete, short-term basis in return for some consideration. This arrangement is ordinarily a developmental dead end, however. It is not suited to permanent contractual relationships, because the "employees" do not remain with one "employer" permanently. Furthermore, the groups concerned are not contractually recruited internally. This form is thus unlikely to lead to a further expansion of contractual principles. It is, moreover, less likely than other contractual forms to enjoy the technical efficiencies ordinarily inherent in contractual work, as initial membership in the employee group is predetermined on noncontractual, social grounds.

Perhaps the best-known organization of this type is the Dahomean *dokpwe*. The *dokpwe* consists primarily of younger men in the community who cooperate in bride-work, although all able-bodied men can on occasion be summoned to help, and membership is reported to run as high as 100. The *dokpwe* is headed by the *dokpwega*, whose office is hereditary, and who is assisted by three subordinates: the *asifaga*, who is in charge specifically of work projects; the *legede*, who is responsible for discipline and attendance at work and other functions; and the *agutapa*, who acts as spokesman and chief of the *dokpwe* at non-work ceremonial functions in which the *dokpwe* is also regularly involved. In fact, the *dokpwe* is only partly a work organization; it also serves many ceremonial functions, and simply, in effect, hires itself out for work from time to time. In order to engage the *dokpwe*, one proceeds to the *dokpwega* with a bottle of liquor, four yards of cloth, and 2 fr. 50, whereupon the *dokpwega* instructs the *legede* to have the members present at the appointed time and place, ready for work. The employer also must agree to pay the workers with a meal of "as rich and varied fare as possible." [9]

Such "ascriptive group employee" contractual arrangements are quite common in traditional societies. Among the Crow Indians of North America, the group employed is a military or religious society; among the Zuni, a fraternal association.[10] The significant fact about such groups is that they remain internally ascriptive despite their contractual agreement as a whole with an employer, and hence enjoy limited developmental potential; the work is, for many of them, essentially a sideline. They should not be confused with guilds, which are also often employed as groups under a contractual arrangement, but which actually function more as businesses performing services for customers than as social groups that

[9] Melville J. Herskovits, *Dahomey* (New York: J. J. Augustin, 1938), pp. 63-77.
[10] Robert H. Lowie, *The Crow Indians*, 23rd Annual Report, Bureau of American Ethnology (Washington, D.C.: Government Printing Office, 1904), p. 350.

also hire themselves out to do work from time to time. We shall have more to say about guilds presently.

Mutual associations. The second of these protocontractual arrangements resembles a contractual extension of the rotational form of reciprocity, though it is not clear that it actually originates in this way. We shall call it a "mutual association," for that is just what it is. A number of persons set up a voluntary association for the purpose of coping with a mutual problem, on the basis of some explicit agreement specifying the work to be done by each member and what he is to receive in return. The crucial difference between this form and rotational reciprocity is that here the association is identified as a corporate body with a concrete identity of its own. There is no external employer; the mutual association itself in effect employs its members, and is often additionally empowered to conclude contractual arrangements for work by others, and, sometimes, to sell shares in the benefits of the work for money or various other considerations. Mutual associations often appear in connection with the construction and maintenance of irrigation works, as for example among the Ifugao of the Philippines and the Chiru of Eastern India, with the latter group also employing this form to cultivate communal village land.[11] Occasionally, mutual associations become quite elaborate. The traditional Burmese had a cooperative method of fishing called *in,* entailing the work of up to a hundred fishermen working the same trap, gathering the fish from it in organized rotating shifts of eight or nine men each. Each member contributed an equivalent amount of money and work, with four or five elders in charge who supervised, collected money, bought necessary equipment, and kept accounts.[12] At first glance, the mutual association form would appear to be developmentally fertile. It is in principle permanent, fully contractual, and often quite autonomous, and can achieve considerable complexity and sophistication. But however "modern" this form may appear on the surface, it seems in fact to possess very limited development potential because its appearance is almost always confined to small landholders or lower-class people in a larger society where the dominant form of work is political. Its possible diffusion is thus typically constrained by an over-all superstructure of politically forced labor. The Chiru example alluded to above is a case in point; the mutual association, called a *lam,* is confined to vil-

[11] Irving Goldman, "The Ifugao of the Philippine Islands," in *Cooperation and Competition among Primitive Peoples,* ed. Margaret Mead (New York: McGraw-Hill Book Company, 1937), pp. 153-79; J. C. Das, "Some Notes on the Economic and Agricultural Life of a Little Known Tribe on the Eastern Frontier of India," *Anthropos,* XXXII (1937), 446-49.

[12] Kenneth G. Orr, *Field Notes on the Burmese Standard of Living* (Rangoon: Department of Anthropology, University of Rangoon, 1951), pp. 14-18.

lagers cultivating village land on the suffrance of the community authorities.[13]

Both the ascriptive group employee type and the mutual association form of contractual work organization do enjoy some advantages of efficiency over both reciprocity and political labor. However, where the authorities are free to appropriate any increase in productivity, and where forced labor is plentiful, considerations of efficiency are unlikely to be of serious importance to any stratum of society involved. Both of these types are hence likely to be "stillborn," insofar as the development of dominant contractual work is concerned, though they can result in a seemingly high incidence of contractual work. Table 3.2 summarizes the over-all situation.

Table 3.2

Type of Society and Type of Socially Determined Work

Type of society	Type of socially determined work			
	Familial only	Familial with reciprocity	All contractual	Political
I and II	0	5	7	1
III	15	26	31	14
IV	5	22	21	33
V	3	13	27	35

Individual contracts. The rather severe reciprocity-cum-forced-labor situation portrayed earlier is thus in practice often moderated by some contractual work, but of a type unproductive of future development. The type of contractual work that can lead somewhere is unfortunately not too common in traditional society, although it happens to be very familiar to us; namely, a situation in which someone simply hires other people to work for him for pay. This type of arrangement has developmental possibilities. In the first place, it produces an organization composed of an aggregate of individuals, rather than an already constituted well-knit group. It thus moves the work organization a step away from social determination, allows for the development of a distinctively organizational culture, and makes possible the enhancement of technical efficiency. Second, this form is at least ecologically suited to permanent institutionalization. Once established, it is thus in a rather favorable competitive position vis-à-vis reciprocal work, with which it often does

[13] *Anthropos,* XXXII, 446-49.

compete in the same social setting. The problem is that it is rather difficult for this type of arrangement to develop as a dominant form; in traditional society, it is most frequently reported as an adjunct to reciprocity rather than a realistic consistent alternative to it. It must compete with both forced labor and reciprocity, both of which forms are usually preferred when they are possible. Once established, this form is often not ineffective in competing with reciprocity, simply because it is, by and large, more efficient. Foster presents an interesting comparison of the technical efficiency of reciprocal and individual contractual work in a rural Mexican community, where he was able to observe both methods employed in the same task. The task was, to be sure, a simple one (the setting of fence posts), but because it was simple, efficiency was easily measured, and he concluded that the contractual method was roughly six times more efficient than the reciprocal system. Foster further observes that the reciprocal system ("voluntary communal," in his terminology) was preferred because everybody had a good time; while the contractual method was viewed merely as a way of getting the job done. Nevertheless, if the main interest was in getting the job done, there was no confusion as to which was the more efficient way to do it.[14]

Forced Labor

If reciprocity is recognized, however grudgingly, as being less efficient than contractual work, forced labor is another matter entirely. The only circumstance in which forced labor is likely to yield to contractual work as a dominant form is where labor that can be recruited by political means is in short supply. Such a situation can result either from a drying up of some established source of forced labor, or from a dearth of centralized political power, or both. In the face of such conditions, the only alternative to a breakdown of the entire work system is the introduction of paid contractual workers. Yet this alternative is apt to be quite unstable, particularly if the economy is not highly commercialized. Furthermore, the combination of a stable government admitting of the possibility of forced labor, a shortage of a forced labor supply, and an adequate supply of contractual labor is not too probable. The result is that paid contractual work seldom becomes established without also entailing political elements. It may emerge not so much as a planned means of recruitment as a last-ditch combination of bribery and threats designed to "keep 'em down on the farm," exhibiting peculiar combinations of forced labor and contract. The history of the Roman *latifundia* from the second century B.C. until well into the Imperial era illustrates a series of

[14] George M. Foster, *A Primitive Mexican Economy* (New York: J. J. Augustin, 1942), p. 34.

shifts from forced labor to contractual work and back again, during which fluctuation it is safe to say that virtually everything was tried, with widely varying degrees of success. Until the second century B.C., free wage labor was widely used, but it became hard to secure because of the growing demands of military conscription. This problem was solved by wars bringing captive slaves, who were then recruited as forced labor. As work became more complex, and as the availability of captive slaves fluctuated, wages were introduced. At the same time such labor remained compulsory, though if a slave saved his money, he could buy his freedom. Discontent was rampant, and was marked by periodic revolts, as well as collusion between slave supervisors and their subordinates in "stalling" on the job. In the first century A.D. a variety of reforms were attempted. Captive slaves were no longer adequate to the demand for labor, and a curious combination of increased pay plus more repressive measures was undertaken. In addition, some freed slaves were settled as tenants, and others, as part of a species of contractual arrangement, were established as serfs. After the time of Augustus, the gradual cessation of foreign conquests resulted in cutting off the supply of slaves entirely, and itinerant free laborers were employed. However, during the later Imperial era there was a growing tendency for the free tenants to become serfs through becoming indebted to landlords, thus being subject to peonage, and ultimately thus reverting again to political labor.[15]

This cycle of forced labor returning ultimately to forced labor via contractual work for pay, indebtedness, peonage, and finally serfdom has been observed elsewhere as well, notably in tribal Iran, where variations in the power of the central government to requisition labor have played an important part in producing fluctuations in the system. A similar pattern has been observed in vestiges of the plantation economy in the southern United States.[16]

Requisites of Contractual Work

The emergence and persistence of contractual work as the dominant basis of work organization in any stable traditional society is thus a rather

[15] Max Cary, A History of Rome (London: Macmillan and Co., Ltd., 1935), pp. 259-60, 451-52, 561-62, 666ff.; William E. Heitland, Agricola (Cambridge: Cambridge University Press, 1921), pp. 151ff.; H. F. Pelham, Essays on Roman History (Oxford: Clarendon Press, 1911), pp. 300ff.

[16] Ann K. Lambton, Landlord and Peasant in Persia (London: Oxford University Press, 1953), pp. 4-7, 120; John Dollard, Caste and Class in a Southern Town, 3rd ed. (Garden City, N.Y.: Doubleday & Company, Inc., 1957), p. 110; also see Raymond Firth, Malay Fishermen (London: Kegan Paul, Trench, Trubner, 1946), pp. 47-93; Richard L. Bowen, Jr., "The Dhow Sailor," The American Neptune (Salem, Mass.), IX (1951), 161-202.

difficult matter. Some of the conditions it requires appear virtually to be mutually exclusive, particularly as regards labor supply and political power.

Labor supply and political power. Contractual work depends on a persistent shortage of forced labor, yet at the same time requires an adequate supply of labor that can be recruited contractually. Such a combination of conditions virtually requires a partially disorganized social setting at the outset, though we shall see that with commercialization this situation can change later. Central political power must be too weak to support large-scale forced labor, yet stable enough to render possible the conclusion and enforcement of work contracts. A typical situation of this variety is one in which some natural disaster or political event has resulted in uprooting significant numbers of people from traditional communities. The consequence is a relatively disorganized migrant labor force, with which there exists no grounds for reciprocal arrangements, which cannot be apprehended for forced labor, but which is available for contractual work.[17]

Reward system. All contractual labor depends upon the presence of a further condition—a reward system that can replace general social obligations as an effective means of motivating work. A person will perform work only if he perceives it to be an effective means to some personal goal. In the case of familial and political work, performance itself is a direct means for fulfilling some social obligation and avoiding the sanctions attached to its nonfulfillment. With contractual work the situation is more complex. Because the social content of contractual relationships is restricted, rewards must be explicitly introduced. A *reward,* in this context, is any object or state of affairs beyond the discharge of a social obligation deemed desirable by a worker and accruing to him as a result of participating in a work organization. Rewards in this sense are not necessarily absent in noncontractual forms of work. They are extremely common in production determined organization, where typically they consist of some share in the product. However, this is an extremely simple situation, and as such is virtually a special case. Production of the product is a generally accepted social goal, which is merely shared by the participants when it is achieved; there is no problem of motivation resulting from a divergence of organizational objectives from personal goals.

Rewards are likewise very common in reciprocity situations, quite apart from any exchange of reciprocal obligations, but are almost universally a relatively minor adjunct. The party for whom the work is being done

[17] See for example S. C. Dube, *Indian Village* (Ithaca, N.Y.: Cornell University Press, 1955), pp. 78-79.

may, for example, give a feast, or otherwise reward the workers with food, after the work is done. The main motivating force is not the reward, but the creation or fulfillment of reciprocal work obligations.

In the case of contractual work, the situation is entirely different. Since general social obligations to participate are minimal, motivation to work is dependent upon rewards, which usually are necessarily different from the product. Production objectives do not constitute general social goals, so there is no guarantee that any promised distribution of shares in them would have any motivational significance. Such distribution may, in fact, be socially or even physically impossible. If a house is being built for a family, the people hired to help build it are not going to be able to live in it too. Besides being different from the product itself, the reward also must have motivational significance and, of course, be capable of being distributed. Money, as we know, does have these characteristics, but other rewards do too, and the presence of a monetary economy is not at this stage of economic development essential to contractual work. Food, as a matter of fact, is the most commonly observed reward in traditional contractual arrangements, and other goods in kind are used as well.

Commercialization. Although a commercialized monetary economy may not, strictly speaking, be essential to the initial appearance of individual contractual work, it seems essential to its continued persistence in the face of the mechanisms we have described that tend to produce a reversion to forced labor. Actually, individual contractual work in traditional society, where it does exist on anything approaching a large scale, reflects a delicate balance between forced recruitment and the labor market mechanism. Both forced labor and contractual labor are usually more or less available in any concrete situation, and the same people may actually be involved in both, where potential employees are in varying states of political dependency and peonage.

The greater the extent of commercialism, the less likely is a total reversion to political work organization; commercialization renders contractual work more competitive with political alternatives in the same setting. At the same time, total removal from politically organized work, or political elements in contractually organized work, is undoubtedly impossible in any society, including modern industrial settings. One of the enduring lessons of Karl Marx has been that economically based contractual relationships always entail some political content, though the relative emphases on contract and politics may vary radically from one setting to another. But some kind of balance is always struck, and from the standpoint of continuing development of contractual principles, that balance must be sufficiently in favor of contractual elements in the context of a commercial exchange system that contractual work ultimately loses its dependence on a continuing shortage of wholly forced labor.

FROM SOCIAL TO TECHNOLOGICAL DETERMINATION

Disengagement from the Social Setting

Given the stable presence of socially determined contractual work in traditional society, under what circumstances and through what processes does it change into technologically determined work? This transformation depends on the properly timed arrival of various external conditions, and the interplay of these conditions with existing contractual work forms. The result of this interplay is a progressive narrowing of the scope of possible social influences on work, combined with the development of a specifically technological focus on the part of the work organization, ultimately yielding technological determination. The entire process can be traced through three stages: *employer-specific contracts, job-specific contracts,* and *occupationally based contracts.* A work contract is employer-specific if a worker, or group of workers, agrees to perform diffuse services for some party in return for some reward. In a *job-specific* arrangement, the worker performs explicitly specified services as well as having a specific employer. An *occupationally based* contract is similar to a job-specific contract, except that workers are recruited at least in part by virtue of their identification with recognized occupations embodying the specific tasks to which they are to be assigned. Occupationally based forms thus lay the foundation for a transition to technological determination.

Each successive stage represents a progressive disengagement from the social setting, and consequently leads to a more rational, and hence more efficient, mode of work organization, as Table 3.3 shows. There is, however, nothing inevitable about this pattern of change. Development from

Table 3.3

Stage of Contractual Organization and Degree of Rationality

Contractual organization	Degree of rationality *			
	0	1	2	3
Employer-specific	4	11	9	0
Job-specific	0	1	2	8
Occupationally based	0	0	3	3

* See p. 54, above, for definition.

one stage to another is contingent upon the presence of appropriate contextual conditions and their interplay with work organization. Furthermore, change from one stage to another does not mean that the forms of work characteristic of the preceding stage cease to exist. They continue to be present alongside the newer forms, though they may decline in relative social importance. The pattern of change is more that of a cumulative scale than a series of transformations. This over-all pattern of tendencies is reflected in Table 3.4.

Table 3.4

Type of Society and Stage of Contractual Organization

Type of society	Stage of contractual organization		
	Employer-specific	Job-specific	Occupationally based
I and II	3	0	0
III	11	6	1
IV	6	5	1
V	9	4	6

Structural Types of Contractual Organization

The classification of contractual organizations as employer-specific, job-specific, or occupationally based is both cross-cut by and empirically related to an important structural typology of contractual organization. Contractual organizations with an ascriptive core—such as a family—employing additional workers on a contractual basis may be distinguished from those of a corporate nature, in which the employer is an individual or a contractually constituted group of people. The former type may, in turn, be subdivided into two types, which we have already identified: the case where the employees form a group that is already internally ascriptively constituted, and the case where the employees are recruited as individuals. The corporate form may similarly be subdivided into mutual associations, which we have already discussed, and another form which we shall call the *corporate business*. Unlike the mutual association, a corporate business is operated by the employer primarily for his (or its) own benefit, with workers paid for their services. It is evident that this type is identical in basic structure to the typical modern industrial firm—not only under conditions of capitalism, but also under conditions of industrial socialism and communism.

One might object to our assertion that such organizations are operated for the benefit of the employer, and without propounding managerial ideology too eloquently, we may readily concede that employees and customers, not to mention the general public, are very likely to benefit considerably from the operation of any corporate business, sometimes even more than the employer does. But in contrast to the case of the mutual association, where a sharing of benefits among the members is paramount, it is the benefit to the employer that remains the ultimate governing force in managerial decisions. We thus may distinguish four structural types of contractual work organization: the ascriptive employer-ascriptive group employee type, the mutual association, the ascriptive employer-individual employee type, and the corporate business. Table 3.5 shows

Table 3.5

Stage and Structural Type of Contractual Organization

Structural type

Stage	Ascriptive core-ascriptive group employee	Mutual association	Ascriptive core-individual employee	Corporate business
Employer-specific	9	4	15	0
Job-specific	0	10	3	2
Occupationally based	0	0	1	7

the relationship of these types to our three stages of contractual development.

We notice, first of all, that there are neither very many corporate businesses nor very many occupationally based contractual situations in preindustrial work, a fact that generally confirms our contention that preindustrial forms of organized work are not, by and large, ready and waiting for application to modern industrial situations. Such corporate businesses as exist in traditional society are, however, either occupationally based or at least job-specific. In contrast, the first two structural types, which we characterized earlier as developmental dead ends, do appear to be just that; with the exception of a few mutual associations, they do not progress beyond the employer-specific level. The ascriptive employer-individual employee form, however, does indeed appear to be developmentally fertile, as we had supposed; it occurs at all three stages of contractual development.

From this preliminary summary we therefore conclude that our three developmental stages are probably realistic; that progression from one stage to the next is, however, contingent on certain as yet unspecified external conditions; and that such a progression, when it occurs, results in a disengagement from social structure reflected both in enhanced efficiency as well as corporate structural forms. Hence it lays a foundation for a transformation to technologically determined work. Let us now examine the dynamics of this progression, and the necessary conditions surrounding it, in greater detail.

EMPLOYER-SPECIFIC AND JOB-SPECIFIC ARRANGEMENTS

Employer-specific Contracts

Employer-specific contracts, by limiting the employer to a specific party rather than an entire potential class of persons, narrow slightly the scope of possible social influences on work. They also serve to engender a slight technological focus by tying the receipt of a reward directly to participation in work. However, they do not go sufficiently far in either direction to differ markedly from many noncontractual forms in these respects. It remains for job-specific contracts to take a major step in introducing some really effective degree of rationality into what still remains a socially determined work situation. By specifically defining and delimiting the worker's job, this type of arrangement greatly narrows the extent of his diffuse obligations to his employer. Furthermore, defining the job not only draws attention to technology, but also provides a basis for varying rewards both according to type of job and quality of performance, thus potentially achieving an even greater commitment to the technical aspects of work.

Job-specific Contracts

Job-specific contractual arrangements arise under the impetus of a relatively complex technology under conditions of a differentiable reward system. Under such circumstances they tend to develop from certain employer-specific forms, and sometimes directly from political forms. Once this type has been established in this way, it can then assume certain other forms of its own. Mutual associations and ascriptive employer-individual employee contractual arrangements can be either employer-specific or job-specific, and the former can develop into the latter. It is very doubtful that ascriptive employer-ascriptive group employee types can develop from an employer-specific to a job-specific state, since the ascriptive internal constitution of the employee group virtually rules out the possibility that an employer could impose upon it a designed set of specific roles; no such cases were found in our sample. Forced labor organizations can, under certain circumstances, develop into contractual job-specific mutual associations, and perhaps into contractual corporate businesses. However, contractual corporate businesses seem more likely to arise by themselves, once job-specific principles of organization have been relatively well established elsewhere in the society.

The simplest transitional case is that of the employer-specific contractual organization confronted by a technology requiring more role differentiation than is readily provided by the social distinctions already existing among the employees. This problem is particularly likely to arise where employees have been hired on an individual basis in a context of sufficient social disorganization to blur ascriptive distinctions among them.[18] Here, even if the technology is relatively simple, it falls to the work organization itself to institutionalize its own structure of role differentiation.

Developing a distinctive role structure becomes a more acute problem with a complex technology. Mutual associations are particularly likely to face this difficulty, since they often arise in response to problems that are rather complex and also somewhat independent of the dominant social structure. However, any technology that is complex relative to social structure requires some planned division of labor and coordination beyond social content already inherent in the recruitment process, if work is to proceed. The usual pattern arising under socially determined conditions is recruitment by general class or caste distinctions, which serve to sort the work force in a preliminary way. At this point, the work organization adds specific job specifications of its own.[19] This step opens up an entirely new realm of possibilities. Within the context of the initial class and caste distinctions as a baseline, so to speak, the organization is then relatively free to reshuffle its entire structure of roles and personnel, relative to technological considerations.[20]

Some organizations can accomplish such reshuffling more easily than

[18] See Walter Elkan, *Migrants and Proletarians* (London: Oxford University Press, 1960).

[19] See, for example, Firth, *Malay Fishermen*, pp. 98-100; Alan H. Brodrick, *Little Vehicle* (London: Hutchinson & Co. (Publishers) Ltd., 1948), p. 149; René Maunier, *La Construction collective de la Maison en Kabylie* (Paris: Institut d'Ethnologie, 1926).

[20] See A. K. Rice, *Productivity and Social Organisation: the Ahmedabad Experiment* (London: Tavistock Publications, 1958).

others. The extent to which any organization can do so depends upon the scope and severity of the social conditions governing initial recruitment, as well as the capacity of the organization to generate institutionalized roles. One example of a social form that operates to facilitate job-specific development, and then functions equally as vigorously to restrain or even prevent further development, is a guild system. A guild is essentially a social group having an institutionalized monopoly on the performance of certain specified work activities. Where guilds exist, it is thus very easy for contractual organizations to recruit members on the basis of general social categories, which are, in themselves, virtually job-specific. In many Southeast Asian societies, for example, canoes have traditionally been constructed by guilds functioning in effect as job-specific corporate businesses. Similarly, in dwelling construction, it is not uncommon for a "master builder" to be called in, who brings apprentices and assistants with him and directs their work. However, inasmuch as guilds are prestructured, they are not ordinarily readily amenable to organizational innovation and restructuring.[21]

Conditions Essential to Job Specificity

Differentiable rewards. Insofar as the capacity of the work organization to generate its own institutionalized roles is concerned, the character of the reward system is extremely important. If a job-specific structure is to develop at all, the reward system must be *differentiable* to at least some degree, and the more differentiable it is, the more pervasive the structure of job specificity is likely to be. By a *differentiable reward system* we mean a situation wherein distinctive amounts of rewards are meaningfully distinguishable.

Where this condition obtains, the work organization can institutionalize its own role structure, simply by attaching different rewards to different roles. The problem solved by differential rewards is both motivational and cognitive. The employer can evoke differing degrees of motivation according to the organizationally perceived importance of the job by offering greater rewards. The cognitive problem is more subtle. If no social basis exists for organizational role differentiation, it is apt literally to be invisible to the participants. Investing different roles with different

21 Walter G. Ivens, *The Island Builders of the Pacific* (London: Seely, Service, 1930), pp. 48-50; also Walter G. Ivens, *Melanesians of the Southeast Solomon Islands* (London: Kegan Paul, Trench, Trubner, 1927), pp. 149-54; C. Daryll Forde, *Habitat, Economy, and Society* (New York: E. P. Dutton & Co., Inc., 1934), p. 215; Margaret Mead, ed., *Cooperation and Competition among Primitive Peoples* (New York: McGraw-Hill Book Company, 1937), p. 289.

rewards has the effect precisely of making the role differences visible. Job-specific contracts, therefore, cannot be made either motivationally or institutionally meaningful in the absence of differentiable rewards.

Commercialization. In principle, any reward that can vary in quantity is differentiable. For all practical purposes, however, the only highly differentiable rewards are those involving the use of money as a general medium of exchange. Thus a commercial economy in which money is used as a reward for work is an essential condition to the development of job-specific contractual arrangements of any practical consequence. To be sure, restricted job-specific arrangements are possible using goods in kind as rewards, for to some extent differing quantities of goods in kind are differentiable in socially significant ways. A few cases in our sample of job-specific contractual organizations employ goods in kind as rewards; but such arrangements are very limited in their possibilities. They are likely to be quite inflexible insofar as future possible reorganizations of work are concerned, and they also offer fewer possibilities of instituting differential rewards based on performance or achievement, an opportunity offered by job-specific arrangements provided the reward system is adequate. Thus the greater the degree of commercialization of the economy, and the more widespread the use of money as a reward for work, the greater the possible scope of job-specific contracts in work organizations, and the greater the potentiality of job-specific arrangements for further development.

Literacy. A further condition, which is not essential to employer-specific contracts but which seems essential to job-specific contracts, at least on a scale sufficient to change the character of organized work, is widespread literacy. Wholesale generation of roles by work organizations themselves requires the design of a system of jobs that is, in its precise form, not a part of the general culture. Such a system presumably cannot be very complex unless it can be written down and read, inasmuch as it must be transmitted to a relatively large number of people who are unfamiliar with it, and who are subject to turnover as well. Certainly, if job-specific organizations are to be very large, literacy is essential to their support and thus at this point becomes essential to the development of large-scale industrial work organizations.

The role of literacy in industrial development has, to be sure, always been recognized, but has sometimes been underestimated. It has usually been discussed in connection with commercialization, where it is found in a similar way to be essential to contracts and complex financial arrangements. Its role in organizational design is perhaps even more evident. Pointing out that European Protestants were traditionally more literate than European Catholics, Stinchcombe goes so far as to suggest that literacy may well be a hidden variable in Weber's theory of the Protestant Ethic, of more importance than the Protestant Ethic itself.[22]

Problems of Reciprocity and Forced Labor

We have portrayed both reciprocity and forced labor as major competitors with contractual organization, particularly at the employer-specific stage. With complex technologies they become somewhat less competitive, because they lack the capacity to become job-specific. Familial organizations without reciprocity are simply not large enough to cope with complex technologies. Reciprocity systems as such do not possess reward structures adequate to the institutionalization of large numbers of specific jobs. There is some indication that under conditions of commercialization, reciprocity systems may tend to turn into contractual mutual associations when confronted with complex technologies, and in this way cope with the problem of job specificity. Three instances appear in our sample, which we coded as "rotational reciprocity," but which we might defensibly have coded as mutual associations. As indicated previously, most reciprocal labor entails rewards in kind, which, however, are actually quite incidental to the situation. In these instances, it was unclear that these rewards were really incidental; they seemed perhaps to be vying with the principle of reciprocal rotation for motivational importance. These cases may represent transitional states. All occur under conditions of relatively complex technology, and it appears that otherwise institutionally undifferentiated roles in these organizations are differentiated by rewards, with some resultant job specificity.

The evidence is somewhat clearer with respect to political organization. Actually, forced labor systems can themselves achieve a limited degree of job specificity by purely political means. Jobs can simply be assigned by those in charge, and performance secured by force; but the purely cognitive problem of differentiating roles still remains. Furthermore, force cannot be calibrated according to achievement so readily as money, not to mention the fact that force is probably unlikely to bring about a really high level of cooperation in any culture. Thus when job specificity is required, purely political work organizations are quite inflexible. Some job specificity is possible (and, as our data have shown, actually results in a modest increase of efficiency on the part of political organizations at this stage), but it cannot be of very great scope, and it is never sufficient to render possible a total realignment of organization structure on a technological basis. Forced labor at this point thus reaches

[22] Arthur L. Stinchcombe, "Social Structure and Organizations," in *Handbook of Organizations*, ed. James G. March (Chicago: Rand McNally & Company, 1965), pp. 150-51.

a dead end. If, however, a relative weakening of centralized political power occurs at this juncture, combined with a shortage of forced labor, it is possible for political work organizations to change to contractual mutual associations, or perhaps, corporate businesses.

The history of San Blas Cuna Indians provides an interesting example of this type of situation. European conquest weakened the local political structure and introduced some degree of commercialization, apparently just when agriculture techniques became more complex. Forced labor thus became somewhat attenuated; participants in *corvées*, for instance, were no longer required to be present on each separate occasion when called, but were simply expected to appear most of the time. To assure such appearance, and in the absence of sufficient force to compel it, contracts were entered into with workers specifying payment for performing specific jobs on particular occasions. The upshot, in agriculture, was a contractual job-specific mutual association, generally supervised by community political leaders. Such units performed other types of work as well, such as construction of walls and houses, for "customers" who paid the organization for its services. The ultimate result, therefore, was no longer a traditional forced labor system, but something very closely akin to a modern socialistic contractual corporate business.[23] It should be pointed out, however, that if the transition to contractualism is not made by political work organizations at this particular point, it may be impossible later on without serious social disruption, given an occupationally based labor recruitment system. For this reason, "socialism" can have widely varying meanings in newly developing areas. In the absence of well-established principles of job specificity, it can mean nothing more than the reestablishment of a traditional forced labor system, with all its attendant disadvantages, including its "dead end" character. If, on the other hand, job specificity is well established, socialistic versions of the new nationalism in developing areas can mean contractual work and further development potential.

Conclusion

Thus the advent of complex technology under conditions of commercialization and fairly widespread literacy is likely to result in job-specific contractual work organization, if employer-specific work of the individual contract or mutual association variety is well established. It is also pos-

[23] Leon S. DeSmidt, *Among the San Blas Indians of Panama* (Troy, N.Y., 1948), pp. 53-56; David B. Stout, *San Blas Cuna Acculturation*, Viking Fund Publications in Anthropology, No. 9 (New York: Viking Fund, 1947); also compare Jean Goudal, *Labour Conditions in Indo-China*, International Labour Office, Studies and Reports, Series B, No. 26 (Geneva: International Labour Office, 1938), p. 28.

sible for political work organizations to change into job-specific contractual forms under similar conditions, if forced labor is in short supply. Job-specific organizations of the individual contract variety, as well as corporate businesses, are capable of further development into occupationally based systems. Mutual associations in traditional society probably are not, owing to the context in which they usually exist and the ways in which they are ordinarily oriented to it.

OCCUPATIONALLY BASED CONTRACTS AND
TECHNOLOGICALLY DETERMINED WORK ORGANIZATION

Organized Work and Occupational Structure

The shift from job-specific contractual organization to occupationally based contractual organization is a critical one, both for the development of technologically determined work organization and for the increased efficiency and industrial adaptability of remaining socially determined forms. This shift depends upon a subtle interplay between job-specific organizations and their social setting and depends on how highly developed the principle of job specificity is, as well as on how widespread job-specific organizations are in the society concerned. Such a shift, therefore, often does not occur, since job-specific organizations frequently remain only partially developed. It is very common in traditional society to find job specificity confined to only a few positions in the organization structure requiring special skills. Construction work is a case in point; it is very commonplace for such activities as stonemasonry and carpentry to be job-specific, with the rest of the organization remaining employer-specific. Only where commercialization is highly developed, and technology already quite complex, is job specificity likely to become sufficiently generalized that the entire organization begins to break away from its essentially socially determined structure.

For this process to persist, it is further essential that it be relatively widespread over many work organizations throughout the entire society. Where such is the case, the groundwork is laid for the development of an occupational structure that can serve as an eventual basis for contractual recruitment. In effect, these conditions lead to a reversal of direction in the causal relationship between work organization and social setting, as portrayed in our model. The advent of similar kinds of work positions in large numbers of job-specific work organizations leads to a situation in which anyone qualified to fill one of these positions in one organization is also qualified to fill similar positions in other organizations. As this possibility becomes increasingly visible, the job structure of work organizations begins to exert an effect on the structure of the social setting, rather than the other way around as indicated by our initial model. Organizational work positions acquire a general social identity and become positions in the general status structure of the society.

The groundwork has already been laid for this development by recruitment in terms of general social categories in job-specific situations. These categories become further broken down into occupationally defined positions, which acquire roughly the same status as the broader category of which they are initially a part. The result is not only the development of an essentially technologically defined labor force, but the investment of the social structure with technologically based distinctions. It then becomes possible for socially determined contractual work organizations to recruit in terms of occupational categories, which are both socially and technologically significant.[24] In a sense, social and technological structure become merged; technological skills are defined by distinctive social statuses; the society in a literal sense becomes, in Ellul's terms, a "technological society." [25]

Industrial technology and job specificity. Such developments are unlikely to take place in the absence of modern industrial technology, which is distinctively characterized by large numbers of relatively standardized jobs. These developments are also unlikely to take place unless modern industrial technology is introduced to a society already extensively characterized by job-specific contractual work organization. In the absence of job specificity, there exists no mechanism through which industrial jobs can be introduced as such into work organizations or can subsequently acquire general social meaning. Furthermore, other things being equal, the widespread introduction of modern industrial technology into an essentially job-specific work structure will, through the process indicated, lead to the development of an industrial occupational structure, and, hence, an industrial labor force. To be sure, this process can be helped along at various points through introducing workers with special skills at critical junctures, but as Moore points out, there are limits to the "exportability of the labor force concept." [26]

To a very great extent, an industrial labor force must develop as a result of interplay between the job requirements of work organizations,

---

[24] See Maunier, *La Construction collective de la Maison en Kabylie;* Wilbert E. Moore, "Changes in Occupational Structures," in *Social Structure and Mobility in Economic Development,* ed. N. J. Smelser and S. M. Lipset (Chicago: Aldine Publishing Company, 1966), pp. 194-212.

[25] Jacques Ellul, *The Technological Society,* trans. J. Wilkinson (New York: Vintage Books, 1964).

[26] Wilbert E. Moore, "The Exportability of the Labor Force Concept," *American Sociological Review,* 18 (1953), 68-72.

the growing visibility of such requirements in the social structure, and the growth of an industrial occupational status system. This development process, however, is unlikely to proceed at a continuous rate, and is apt particularly at this point to be subject to constraint as a result of a general lack of labor mobility and viable urbanization. Such constraints are not only factors in the labor market in the broad sense, but thus emerge as possible obstacles to interplay between organizational and occupational structure.[27]

The Shift to Technolgical Determination

Up to this point, organized work is still, however, socially determined. To be sure, it is apt to be more efficient than traditional socially determined work, because the social structure itself has become more technologically based. The intrinsic properties of our model still remain valid, however, and the work organizations are only indirectly adapting to technological requirements, through the social status structure. Work is therefore likely to remain relatively inefficient by industrial standards. Since it is still oriented to the social setting, it is further likely to lack technological innovative capacity, and thus give the impression of being defective in commitment to the "rational spirit." This impression is valid only in a special sense, however; much activity appears "nonrational" not because the people concerned are incapable of logic, but because they are still primarily not trying to solve technologically defined problems. A continuing orientation to a technologically defined occupational structure, however, draws attention to technological problems per se, and eventually produces at least a partial shift on the part of the work organization to an orientation to technology itself, as a generalized system of knowledge and capabilities, independent of social structure per se. This shift is probably never complete. It is certainly not complete in our own society, and eventually, as we shall see, it is suffused by a tendency toward pluralistic work organization, in which the problem becomes somewhat redefined. Technologically determined work organization is thus perhaps best thought of as a continuing strong tendency, under the conditions we have described.

Occupational Structure and Industrialism

We would thus hold that the most socially significant initial aspect of modern industrialism is its occupational structure, rather than the par-

[27] See for example Elkan, *Migrants and Proletarians;* also Walter Elkan and Lloyd A. Fallers, "The Mobility of Labor," in *Labor Commitment and Social Change in Developing Areas,* ed. W. E. Moore and A. S. Feldman (New York: Social Science Research Council, 1960), pp. 238-57.

ticular hardware, attitudes, or expert knowledge it entails. Furthermore, the development of a fundamentally industrial occupational structure is an essential prior condition to the development of a rational orientation toward industrial facilities, knowledge, and capabilities. It is one thing for technological and scientific knowledge to be culturally available; it it quite another matter for such knowledge and capability to be used effectively as the chief source of organizing principles in work. Such use is gradually built into work organization through the development of an industrial occupational system as a basis for recruitment, and in turn has a snowballing effect on the occupational system.

This process represents the organizational "takeoff" into industrialism and, through time, results both in technologically determined organized work or something very close to it, and in lending a technological cast to the entire social structure. One of the most well-documented and consistent findings of social stratification research, for example, is that general social status in modern industrial society is determined more by occupation than by anything else. Hollingshead, for instance, has quite consistently found in a variety of studies that if all that one knows about a person in American society is his occupation, one can predict his general reputational social standing in the community, and be correct roughly 75 per cent of the time.[28] This situation is not true of traditional society, and it reflects the fact that the aggregated structure of organized work in modern industrial society has an exceedingly strong effect on the structure of the social setting. Ellul terms modern society a "technological society" on the grounds that all problems in it tend to be solved by formal technical paradigms, and that problems that cannot be stated in this way are either reformulated until they can be or ignored altogether.[29]

Actually, the technological character of modern society goes even deeper than Ellul indicates. Because of the primacy of the occupational system, the entire social hierarchy largely resembles an ideal-typical technologically determined work organization. There are, to be sure, occupations that do not fit this model, but it is fairly safe to say that any behavior they involve that cannot be at least indirectly justified technologically is very apt to be considered outside the mainstream of modern life, and is not unlikely to be viewed as downright deviant. Organized work thus occupies a uniquely central place in modern industrial culture. Its organization is strongly technologically determined; the society in which it exists is strongly organizationally determined; and the resultant

[28] A. B. Hollingshead and F. C. Redlich, *Social Class and Mental Illness* (New York: Wiley, 1958), pp. 387-97.
[29] Ellul, *The Technological Society.*

social structure is, to complete the cycle, strongly supportive of technologically determined work.

TIMING AND EXTERNAL INFLUENCES

Our discussion in this chapter, as throughout the book, has focussed
on work organization in particular, rather than on industrial and economic development generally. As a result, many topics familiar to the
student of general economic and industrial development have emerged
in our discussion as "external conditions" rather than as objects of study.
We have thus not been interested in exploring such problems as how
and why a commercialized market economy develops, or even how industrial technology per se, as a system of knowledge and capabilities, comes
into being. Rather, we have tried to point out how, and at what point,
the development of such contextual conditions relates to the development of industrially appropriate forms of work organization. In general,
we have concerned ourselves with the origins of these contextual conditions themselves only insofar as organized work itself plays a significant
part in their causation. This part, however, is often considerable, particularly where occupational structure as a socially significant feature of
modern industrial society is concerned.

Here, as elsewhere, the chain of reciprocal effects between general social, technical, and economic conditions, on the one hand, and work
organization, on the other, is clearly a major mechanism in the over-all
process of economic and industrial development. The contribution of
this part of our discussion should be to reveal such a mechanism as a
major component in the total development process. From this recognition flows the major corollary that the prevailing mode of work organization is a critical intervening variable in determining whether certain
general conditions will actually contribute causally to, not merely facilitate, such development. On this score the timing of the arrival of potential external influences relative to the developmental state of organized
work is crucial in determining whether or not they will actually have any
positive effect on industrial development. If their arrival is premature,
no basis will be present for linkage between them and the work process
itself, and no mechanism will arise through which they can have any
effect. Indeed, sometimes premature arrival of otherwise potentially positive external influences may engender adaptive reactions transforming
them into actually negative influences on the development process. Similarly, the tardy arrival of given external conditions may make it difficult
for them to have any effect on a situation that has had time to become
established on a stable basis.

Direct External Influences

Figure 3.1 illustrates this interplay between the structure of organized work and the external conditions that we have found to be immediately and directly related to it in the development process. To summarize, reciprocity and forced labor appear as responses to variable work loads in traditional socially determined work organization. Shortages of reciprocal and forced labor, if combined with the possibility of reward systems, lead to the development of employer-specific contractual work. At this point, but not prior to it, the advent of complex technologies, combined with a level of commercialization sufficient to result in differentiable rewards, and widespread literacy, tends to result in job-specific contractual organization, mainly from employer-specific sources, but also possibly from political sources if forced labor is in short supply and the government relatively weak. Given a relatively well-established structure of job specificity in work, the introduction of industrial technology at this juncture will be met by reasonably effective adaptations on the part of work organizations, eventually leading to a modern industrial production system. As jobs become increasingly standardized, the structure of organized work begins to exert an effect on occupational structure, giving it a technological basis, enabling it to serve as a foundation for recruitment of workers to jobs, and hence leading to occupationally based contractual work. Finally, occupationally based contractual work, as it becomes widespread, draws attention to the cultural and general structural aspects of technology, and thus generates tendencies toward technologically determined work organization physically appropriate to modern industry.

Secondary Conditions

This model considers only the external conditions that we have found to be directly related to organized work per se. An entire set of secondary conditions also exists, which we have not found to be directly related to work organization, but which have consistently been found to be of general importance to economic development generally, and which interact in significant ways with the more direct external conditions to work.

Let us briefly consider the place of these "secondary conditions"—secondary only from the point of view of work organization as such, and not in general importance—in the scheme we have outlined. We shall consider six of these conditions: general commercialization, geographical mobility, separation of production from consumption, political stability, entrepreneurship, and technological expertise (including the "rational

FIGURE 3.1
The Transition from Socially Determined to Technologically
Determined Work

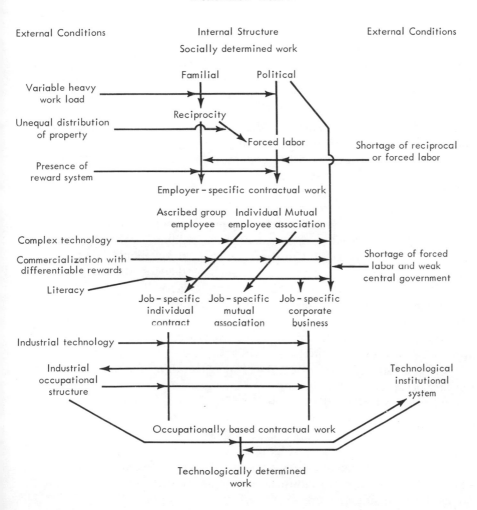

spirit") and facilities. These conditions are widely discussed in the literature on general economic development. It is our purpose to explore their
relationships to the development of organized industrial work per se.

Commercialization and geographical mobility. Some degree of commercialization and potential geographical mobility of population may be
helpful in the development of employer-specific contractual work, though
at this stage neither is wholly essential, as we have seen. Commercialization not only becomes essential, however, if a transition is to be made
to job-specific contracts (and thereafter), but also helps motivate such
a transition directly if at that point production becomes specialized relative to consumption. This specialization is, in turn, contributed to by
growth in employer-specific contracts by virtue of their tendency to
render employees dependent for their consumption upon the production
of others. Geographical mobility of the labor force in response to labor
demand similarly becomes essential to the expansion of job-specific contractual work. Under some circumstances, it may be essential before this
point, if it reflects a breakdown in political and reciprocal recruitment
patterns, leading to migrant labor and providing a potential labor pool
for employer-specific arrangements.

Political stability and entrepreneurship. Political stability and entrepreneurship are of considerable interest because each can either aid or
hinder the process of industrial development, depending on when it appears and the form it takes. Some modicum of political instability would
seem to be positively helpful to the creation of an available labor pool
for employer-specific organizations, for such work depends partly on a
breakdown in traditional methods of recruiting labor by political force.
Furthermore, under conditions of political stability, there exists, as we
have seen, some tendency for employer-specific contractual arrangements
to revert to political forms of work, where power can be consolidated
around the institution of debt peonage.

Given the establishment of employer-specific work, however, political
stability becomes essential if such work is to eventuate in technologically
determined production, through the development of an industrial occupational structure. The reason is that such development requires sustained predictability in the labor market, as well as in the exchange value
of rewards. It also must be possible for the newly emerging occupational
status system to be sanctioned and preserved. Thus the status of political
stability as a condition for industrial development is rather curious, insofar as the demands of work organization are concerned. In the earlier
stages of development it appears that some political instability, possibly
even approaching upheaval, is essential if existing forms of socially determined work are to become undermined to the point of no longer being

competitive with contractual forms. Yet once contractual forms are developed, their capacity to bring about a shift to technologically determined work organization depends, in part, on political stability. It is a question of the replacement of older political forms with their attendant traditional status systems by new ones admitting of a reorganization of the status structure along industrial occupational lines.

A somewhat parallel situation obtains with respect to entrepreneurship. The degree to which an "entrepreneurial spirit" does or does not aid industrial development is a subject of some controversy. The proponents of the entrepreneurial position argue that innovative entrepreneurship, if not absolutely essential to the adoption of an industrial technology, certainly materially assists such adoption. The critics of this position point to a variety of societies that do not lack for vigorous small-scale entrepreneurial activity in commerce and finance, but which certainly appear to be brought no closer to the establishment of large-scale industry as a result of such activity. On the contrary, the complex obligations and economic status structure engendered by multifarious small-scale mercantile enterprises seem at times to militate against the development of a focus on technology, as opposed to commercialization alone.[30]

We would suggest that the proponents and critics are both correct, but that they are referring to different developmental stages of contractual work. Unless a firm basis for industrial development exists in the occupational system, entrepreneurial activity is likely at best to be irrelevant to industrialization, inasmuch as commercial opportunities are unlikely to engender organizations that demand specialized technical skill supportive of an industrial occupational structure. The result is a nation of shopkeepers and clerks, rather than a corps of technicians. A high incidence of entrepreneurial activity where there are only employer-specific contractual arrangements is thus apt to be competitive with, rather than supportive of, the development of job-specific forms amenable to expansion into occupationally based work arrangements. Vigorous small-scale entrepreneurial activity at that stage furthermore can be a major factor in bringing about a pyramidal debt system, which forces existing contractual work into a political mold through peonage. On the other hand, given a relatively firmly established nascent industrial status structure, entrepreneurs will tend to be more technologically oriented, and at this stage entrepreneurial innovation may be expected by and large to be conducive to further industrial development.

[30] See Nash, *Primitive and Peasant Economic Systems*, esp. pp. 58-59. Also of considerable interest on this score is the comparison offered by Clifford Geertz, *Peddlers and Princes: Social Change and Economic Modernization in Two Indonesian Towns* (Chicago: University of Chicago Press, 1963).

Entrepreneurship thus parallels political stability in its effects on organized work, but in certain respects it is more nearly analogous to state intervention in that its effects depend on "when" and "what kind"—with "what kind" to some extent being a function of "when." It is important not to confuse state intervention—or socialism, for that matter—with what we have identified as politically organized work in traditional society. The two are not formally related. It is quite possible, for example, for "private enterprise" to result in politically organized work in our terms, to the extent that it operates through an ascriptive stratification system, as it inevitably does to some extent anywhere. It is likewise perfectly possible for government enterprises to be contractual, to the extent that they recruit people on the basis of explicit agreements, particularly in the context of a standard system of industrial occupations, as they inevitably will in any industrial society. However, it is likely that state intervention, if it occurs prior to the widespread development of job-specific contractual forms, will accelerate a reversion to political work organization in the same way as will vigorous commercial entrepreneurial activity at this stage. In fact, the effect is likely to be even more direct, and colonial powers have at times used this tendency as a means of perpetuating subjugation by controlling development.[31] However, if state intervention occurs later, after job-specific work is well established, provided that older political forms have been replaced by new ones, the state can be an important instrument in mobilizing a transition to industrial production. We shall not expand on this point here, as it has frequently been extensively discussed by others. Suffice it to say that most newly industrializing nations are proceeding more or less through state intervention, and that an important question to raise about it is whether or not the conditions essential to its effectiveness, as just outlined, have been met.

It is also the case that regardless of the maturity of industrial occupational structure and the diffusion throughout the society of industrial technology in the hardware-and-knowledge sense, the conflict between contractual and political principles of organized work never seems fully to be resolved. The technological determination of work is thus never fully complete; there is always some tendency for work to be socially determined. Furthermore, quite apart from family favoritism and the old school tie, elements of forced labor and peonage seem likely to be involved. It matters not whether political bureaucracy replaces the despot, or whether the finance company replaces the landlord. The advent of modern industrial technology never wholly removes the bases of social determination.

[31] See Paul A. Baran, *The Political Economy of Growth* (New York: Monthly Review Press, 1957).

Industrial technology. In conclusion, let us consider the adoption of industrial technology itself in the hardware-and-knowledge sense. If our analysis is correct, such adoption cannot occur in a manner favorable to further growth unless it is concomitant with the development of job-specific work into an industrial occupational structure. If it is attempted before this point, conditions for the motivation of industrial work through contractual labor will be incomplete. The result, from the point of view of the work organization, is likely to be difficulty in recruiting a work force, gross ineffectiveness and inefficiency resulting from the attempted utilization of existing socially determined work forms, or both. Given a government with sufficient political power—indigenous or otherwise—some industrial enterprises can be made to function after a fashion under such circumstances. But the seeds of further growth are not there, and a dead end under rather despotic conditions is virtually assured.

This very process has been a fairly common strategy among colonial powers and has been advocated by advisers to such powers as an effective means of getting much, albeit inefficient, work from the "natives" while giving them a minimum of material benefits, new ideas, or future hopes. This strategy indeed tends to have just such an effect. For bona fide industrial development to occur, suitable work organizations must be developed for it. Such organizations are developed through the feeding of technological hardware, knowledge, and expertise into the system as an industrial occupational structure develops.

CONCLUSION

Mechanisms producing industrial development cannot be adequately described without taking account of the prevailing mode of work organization in the society concerned. Industrial development cannot therefore be ascribed to some set of ideas and attitudes, or to some set of general structural conditions, but comes about through the reciprocal influence of such elements, on the one hand, and ongoing work organizations, on the other. The main organizational transformation that must take place is a shift from socially determined to technologically determined forms of work. Crucial to this shift is the institution of contractual work, its successful competition with familial, reciprocal, and political work forms, and its development through employer-specific and job-specific arrangements to a firm position in a new occupational system grounded in industrial technology. The success of this development depends on the timing and nature of various external influences relative to the stage reached by prevailing forms of work organization. Finally, an industrial occupational system is both an effect, and later a cause, of this development, as the major social embodiment of industrial technology. It provides a combined technological and social basis for industrial work organization.

We now turn to a consideration of the nature and problems of industrial work organization. Our initial model of the work system shows that no work system is ever stable. In this sense, all work systems are in a continuous process of either dissolution or development—and sometimes both. We have seen how this is true of primitive and traditional organized work. It is no less true of organized work in modern industrial society.

One particularly devastating reaction to any highly abstruse exposition of organization theory is the question, "Where do you put the accounting department?" [1] To the proper theoretician, the implication that something so mundane as an accounting department should be mentioned in the same breath with such hallowed concepts as "rational-legal authority," or "multi-level decisional processes" is not only a breach of academic etiquette, but, in the words of Malthus, "a very unphilosophical mode of arguing." [2] The fact is, however, that virtually every large-scale industrial work organization not only has an accounting department but also exhibits other similarly differentiated units with names like "marketing and sales," "production," and "research and development." Brute force induction alone would lead us to suppose that such concepts must therefore be more general than they sound, and hence of more abstract significance than much of modern organization theory makes them appear to be.

We contend that such is indeed the case, the reason being that modern industrial work organization is, unlike preindustrial forms, pluralistic rather than unitary in structure. It is an essential characteristic of modern industrial firms, not only that they be

[1] Charles R. Walker, in numerous vigorous, though perhaps unsuccessful, personal conversations, for which the author is grateful.
[2] Thomas R. Malthus, *Population: the First Essay* (Ann Arbor: Ann Arbor Paperbacks, The University of Michigan Press, 1959), p. 5.

CHAPTER FOUR

The Development of Pluralistic Organization

subdivided into segregated departments, but that the functions of certain of these departments be similar from one firm to another. If this contention is true, the fact that large numbers of industrial organizations possess a group called an "accounting department," differentiated from another group called a "research and development unit," ceases to be a nuts-and-bolts matter, but demands general theoretical consideration.

By and large, organization theory has not accorded this problem that type of consideration. Certainly this is not because organization theory has overlooked the fact of differentiation per se; indeed, in many versions of both classical and modern theory, differentiation, or "departmentalization," occupies a fairly central position.[3] But departmentalization as it exists in modern industry is not ordinarily treated as being generically different from other manifestations of the division of labor. The fact that it exists there is taken to be a necessary consequence of increasing organizational size, and the precise form it assumes in any given organization is deemed to be a function of administrative decisions that take into account the relative advantages deriving from the varying complementarities of possible patterns of specialization.

Departmentalization has thus been most often viewed not so much as a basic organizational characteristic, but rather as a problem of administrative planning offering a variety of options, some of which are better than others, depending on what one is trying to do. The possibility that departmentalization itself, as well as particular patterns of departmentalization, might be generated by mechanisms other than sheer increase in size or purposeful administrative planning has been given very little attention, despite the fact that large numbers of otherwise quite disparate modern work organizations—including some rather small ones—palpably exhibit strikingly similar departmental structures. Furthermore, these similarities cannot be accounted for altogether by the presumption that these various enterprises are all faced with similar economic problems, or the possibility that their administrators all attended the same business school or read the same textbooks on how to organize an industrial concern.

All of this is not to deny that increased organizational size does render some pattern of specialization functionally necessary, or to suggest that none of this specialization is purposely planned. Obviously much of it is. What we are suggesting is that such planning is subject to general constraints that go far beyond considerations of organizational size, and stem ultimately from those inconsistencies intrinsic to work systems that we have outlined. The interplay between these constraints, on the one hand,

---

[3] For a discussion of "classical" theories of departmentalization, see James G. March and Herbert A. Simon, *Organizations* (New York: John Wiley & Sons, Inc., 1958), pp. 22-33.

and the character of both industrial technology and industrial society, on the other, tends not only to generate pluralistic forms of organized work, but pluralistic forms with concretely similar patterns of differentiation. It is thus more than a mere coincidence of planning that "accounting departments," "production departments," and "research and development units" are widespread as specialized concrete entities, often under circumstances that appear radically different from one another.

THE PROCESS OF PLURALISTIC DEVELOPMENT: A THEORY

According to our basic model of organized work, actual relationships among the parts of any work system are always functionally inconsistent. If we assume in addition that no person can be persistently and manifestly oriented in an authentic way to a functionally inconsistent set of relationships, this situation poses problems for the institutionalization of organized work. Specifically, if work is to proceed, its inconsistencies must somehow be concealed by the way in which the work organization is culturally defined. There are two ways, broadly speaking, in which this is possible.

The first is by culturally defining the work system itself as involving consistent relationships only. This solution can assume three forms, which yield, respectively, the production determined, socially determined, and technologically determined forms of organized work which we have so far discussed. These forms function by "mass selective perception," as it were, recognizing only certain consistent relationships in the work system and ignoring others, with the various consequences and implications we have described.

The second possible solution to the problem of inconsistency is pluralistic. A pluralistic work organization is oriented to all basic relationships in the work system despite their functional inconsistencies. This state of affairs is made possible by differentiating the work organization into segregated sub-groups, each of which is oriented to a different set of consistent relationships, with the result that all relationships are covered without any given number being subject to any basic hiatus in role expectations.

We have already shown that production determined work organization is characteristic of highly primitive society, and that as preindustrial society develops, a shift occurs to socially determined forms. We have also shown strong reason to believe that industrialization requires the presence of either technologically determined or pluralistic forms of work organization, and that under certain conditions, pressures toward industrialization will result in a shift from socially determined to technologically determined work. We shall now argue that the mechanics of operation of technologically determined work organizations, in interplay with the social and technological context in which they function, result in the development, under industrial conditions, of pluralistic forms of work organization.

Technologically determined organization, in its "pure" form, is exceedingly unstable. Its major problem is that the technology to which technologically determined work organizations are oriented, is a highly generalized system of knowledge and capabilities, rather than a specific, particular means of achieving given, limited, production objectives. This very general technological system thus does not unequivocally imply either a specific set of production objectives or a specific organization structure. Rather, it is potentially applicable to the achievement of a wide range of production objectives, and capable of expression in a wide range of organizational forms. In order for work to take place, therefore, a choice from among these possible production objectives and organizational forms must somehow be made. No similar problem of choice is present in either production determined or socially determined organizations. In production determined forms, specific production objectives are given at the outset. They imply a fairly specific technology, which in turn admits of only a very narrow range of organizational possibilities. With socially determined forms, the organization structure is given, and this situation immediately narrows the possible range of choice of either technology or production objectives; the members play given roles present in the organization structure, from which roles a technology emerges, which in turn yields production objectives.

With technologically determined work the situation is entirely different. The problem is to choose from among a wide range of physically possible production objectives, and the crux of the matter is that such a choice cannot be made on technological grounds alone. Any social choice must proceed from an ordering of alternatives according to some set of cultural values. Where in this situation do such values come from?

One possibility would be that the work organization not make the choice at all, but that some group in the social setting do so. The image of a government in a newly developing country setting production targets immediately comes to mind. Superficially it would seem that the effect of such a situation would be to turn the work organization into a production determined form, with objectives given at the outset. However, given the complexity of the type of society with which we are concerned here, such a development would be exceedingly unlikely. The potential goal structure of the society would be sufficiently diverse that imposed production objectives would have to be enforced in some way, with the result that the organization would revert to being socially determined. Although this is a real possibility, a complete reversion is very unlikely, given an industrial occupational system, a relatively stable structure of technological institutions, and a highly commercialized economy. It is more realistic to suppose that external political regulation of production objectives would emerge simply as a condition under which the work organization was obliged to function, with the organization itself still remaining strongly implicated in the decision-making process. Such an outcome leads us back, essentially, to our original problem.

Pluralism

Any conceivable way of avoiding organization choice at this juncture, if possible at all, would result in developmental regression of the work organization, most probably to a socially determined form. How then do work organizations go about making a choice of production objectives from among a wide range of alternatives? This process necessarily entails, first, an assessment of the probable impact of one objective as opposed to another on the social setting and the way this impact would be evaluated in the setting. Second, it involves an assessment of the probable consequences to the organization resulting from such evaluation.

The precise difficulties inherent in this decisional process now become evident. The process itself evokes manifest consideration, on the part of the work organization, of the relationships between the social setting, on the one hand, and both production objectives and organization structure, on the other. Our original model tells us, however, that the simultaneous recognition of these two relationships alone, not to mention the already institutionalized direct relationship between the social setting and technology, would be sufficient to introduce inconsistencies into the way the structure of the work organization is culturally defined. We thus conclude that it is impossible for any technologically determined work organization to function as a unit.

What happens? Barring complete dissolution of the organization, and assuming the organization does not revert to being socially determined, the only remaining possibility is that the organization will become pluralistic, that is, differentiated into subunits, themselves oriented to consistent relationships.

We may thus propose the hypothesis that, as work organizations become increasingly technologically determined, they at the same time become differentiated into specialized parts. This differentiation presumably lays the foundation for pluralism. Before we try to confront this hypothesis with data, let us also ask whether we would, on theoretical grounds, expect such differentiation to follow any particular pattern. We conceive all pluralistic work organizations to be differentiated into *departments*, which are oriented either to *sectors* of the work system and its environment, or to relationships with other departments. A *department* is a concretely differentiated subunit of a work organization, having a distinctive membership. By our model, no department can be oriented to an inconsistent set of relationships in the work system.[4] Thus no department can be oriented to more than one sector. It is possible, however, for a department to be oriented to only *part* of one sector since, as we shall see, sectors are in practice frequently subdivided so as to involve more than a single department.

The number of ways in which any work system can be divided into sectors, as well as the number of patterns of departmentalization possible in any pluralistic work organization, would seem, at first thought, to be virtually infinite. However, by assuming that pluralistic work organization develops from technologically determined forms, we can reduce the number of practical possibilities in each case to manageable proportions, and thus make some general inferences about probable sector and departmental structure.

Sectors

It is possible to narrow the field of practical possibilities very considerably with respect to sector structure. In the first place, the work organization itself will necessarily emerge as a component in every sector, since it is the only social unit in the immediate work situation, and hence the only component there capable of orientation and action. Second, some relationship between social setting and technology will likewise appear in every sector, since we are assuming that pluralistic organization develops from technologically determined forms. This same assumption also tells us that technology enters the work system on both a general and a particular level. The work organization is, first of all, oriented to a generalized set of technological possibilities. Having adapted itself to their consideration, it chooses specific production objectives from among the many possibilities allowed by the generalized technology. However, as we have seen, it cannot do this without evaluating the differential impact of

[4] The term "sector" is taken from Paul R. Lawrence and Jay W. Lorsch, *Organization and Environment* (Boston: Division of Research, Graduate School of Business Administration, Harvard University, 1967), p. 29 and *passim*. The actual definition is, however, our own. I am indebted to professors Lawrence and Lorsch, in the work just cited as well as through personal conversations, for many suggestions that have helped me to clarify the concept of pluralistic work organization. Any obfuscation that remains is my fault and not theirs.

possible alternative objectives on the social setting, and estimating the subsequent reaction of the setting as it is felt directly by the work organization. Finally, having chosen a set of specific production objectives, the work organization then adapts a particular technology to their achievement, and its own structure to that particular technology.

This two-level character of technology introduces a further complication into the work system, having implications for sector structure, and also, incidentally, serving along with other mechanisms already described to render pluralism an inevitable consequence of ongoing technologically determined work. For reasons parallel to those advanced in Chapter One regarding the work system as a whole, the three relationships between social setting, particular technology, and general technology present intrinsic inconsistencies of their own. For example, the direct implications of the social setting for particular technology are never the same as the indirect implications of the social setting for particular technology felt via general technology. It is hence impossible for more than two of these relationships to appear in the same sector.

We thus conclude from the foregoing considerations that there will exist three and only three sectors in any pluralistic work organization. Figure 4.1 summarizes the situation, and also illustrates the two-level

FIGURE 4.1

Pluralistic and Technologically Determined
Work Organization and Work System

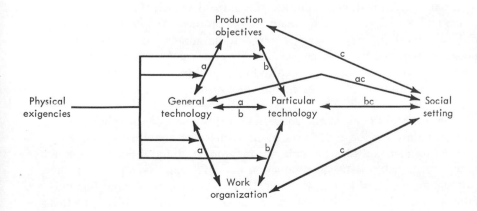

character of technology common to both technologically determined and pluralistic forms.

The scientific sector. The first sector (a), which we shall call the *scientific* sector, comprises relationships between the social setting and general technology, on the one hand, with production objectives, particular technology, and organization structure, on the other. The activities connected with this sector include the assessment of the state of general technological knowledge and capability as given by the social setting, the development of ways of using such knowledge and capability to achieve production objectives, and the maintenance of an organization structure that can perform these functions.

The production sector. The second sector (b) is the *production* sector, which comprises relationships between particular technology, on the one hand, and the remaining components, on the other. As to activities, production involves the fitting of a particular socially and physically available technology to the achievement of a given set of production objectives, and the maintenance of an organization structure appropriate to that particular technology.

The social sector. The third sector (c) will be called the *social* sector; it includes relationships between the social setting, on the one hand, and production objectives, general and particular technology, and the work organization, on the other. Its activities entail the assessment of the probable impact of the states of production objectives, technology on both levels, and organization structure, on the social setting, combined with efforts to control, modify, and offset the effects of evaluation of this impact when deemed necessary. In specific terms these functions can include a very wide range of activities. Some of the most important ones typically include marketing; sales; making decisions about specific production objectives in light of evaluation of market conditions; procurement of raw materials, equipment, and facilities; recruitment of personnel; labor relations; and a variety of public relations operations. Despite the diversity of these functions, they properly emerge in the same sector, since they are not necessarily culturally inconsistent with one another. They would become so, of course, if they also involved relationships between components of the immediate work situation, but they do not as they are ordinarily carried out.

From the standpoint of the social sector, for example, procurement of raw materials can be made consistent with sales activities through an accounting mechanism, which may or may not indirectly result in a consistent relationship between production objectives and technology in the production sector. But if it does not, that fact will not become immediately visible, since two different, segregated, sectors are involved. In this way the organization can, in principle, "live with the problem," even if it is not resolved, simply because the diffusion of knowledge between sectors is incomplete.

Sectors therefore represent complexes of functions deriving from the relationships they represent. In a formal sense, these functions, and hence the sectors themselves, are aspects of organizational action. Sectors, however, are more than analytic aspects. They are also, by our model, concrete entities, with respect to both activities and people. If purposive action is to be maintained, they cannot overlap without serious disruption to the work system.

Departmentalization

This rare concordance of structure and function on the part of the sectors of pluralistically organized work systems permits us to use sector structure as a point of departure for our discussion of departmentalization, and ultimately leads us to see why the question of where the accounting department goes is not theoretically irrelevant. To be sure, we cannot predict from our model the precise pattern of departmentalization in any work organization. We can, nevertheless, indicate certain conditions to which any pattern of departmentalization is subject, and project some probable patterns from these conditions.

In the first place, we may assert that any pluralistic work organization will be differentiated into at least three departments—one oriented to each of the three sectors, respectively. As a practical matter it is likely that more than three departments will emerge in any given case. Although it is impossible for one department to be oriented to more than one sector, it is by no means impossible for further specialization to take place within any given sector, and our model suggests some patterns that such specialization might assume. Each sector involves three basic relationships, which, though consistent with one another, do nonetheless involve essentially different kinds of problems. It thus seems reasonable to suppose that if further departmentalization is going to take place at all, it will likely be based on these differences. One might therefore expect to find, not one "social department," but a subdivision into marketing and sales, procurement, and personnel, as a minimum. These departments would correspond, respectively, to relationships between productive objectives and social setting, technology and social setting, and organization structure and social setting. Similarly, production might well be subdivided into internal operations, internal accounting and control, and production management. It is perhaps not unusual for the scientific sector as a whole to involve a single research and development department, but further subdivision into basic research, engineering, and research administration is not unusual either. In fact, any pattern of departmental differentiation can occur in principle, provided that no one department is oriented to more than one sector.

We would suggest that the most probable pattern is some elaboration of the foregoing, and will later present some findings, which, though fragmentary for our purposes, lend general support to this suggestion. For the present we make two observations. First, the particular sub-divisions we have suggested do in fact resemble actual titles of departments in many industrial firms. Second, the actual functions of departments are unlikely to exhaust all of the potential content of the sector, or sub-sector, to which they are oriented. For example, the typical "marketing and sales" department is certainly not concerned with everything involved in relationships between production objectives and the social setting, though it does reflect a primary strategy in dealing with such relationships in a commercial economy.

There is yet another reason for supposing that departmentalization in any typical pluralistic work organization will be more extensive than sector structure alone would suggest. In addition to being oriented to sectors, departments can be oriented to relationships between other departments, independently of involvement in the sector structure on the part of any department concerned. This possibility—which we shall presently see is always to some extent a certainty—permits the existence of an entire superstructure of interdepartmental concerns and relationships that are not directly involved with sectors at all and that complicate our model considerably. They do not basically alter it, however. It is still impossible for any department to be oriented to more than one sector. However, it is possible for a department to be oriented to relationships between departments as such, which are themselves oriented to different sectors. There is no contradiction between these two statements, provided an orientation to relationships between departments in different sectors is based on some aspect of those departments other than their actual sector activities. An accounting department, for example, can be concerned with reviewing the financial status of other departments without direct regard to their actual activities.

This possibility of orientation to relationships between departments independently of sectors is a critical feature of pluralistic work organization. It not only renders such organizations exceedingly flexible, but also —more basically—makes structural integration possible under pluralistic conditions.

Coordination and Integration

Unlike the unitary forms examined earlier, pluralistic work organizations present potentially monumental problems of integration. In the absence of a pluralistic structure, integrative problems do not go beyond questions of simple coordination of a basically complementary division of labor; but in pluralistic organization, not all of the division of labor is complementary. Departments in different sectors inevitably operate at cross purposes at some point, since the activities involved in different sectors always entail inconsistencies. Furthermore, it is impossible for any integrating unit to be oriented to the different sectors involved, and so simply mediate their requirements. Not only can such conflicting requirements not be mediated, but no integrating unit can be oriented to more than one sector, in any event.

How, then, is integration possible in pluralistic organizations? It is possible by virtue of interdepartmental orientations, apart from orientations to sectors. Either the departments in different sectors can be oriented to one another as departments, or some other department can be oriented to the relationships between the departments to be integrated, or some combination of the two. A striking feature of the situation, though, is that integration of departments in different sectors must take place on grounds other than the actual operations of the departments concerned, for otherwise the integrating unit would be oriented to more than one sector. It is not merely a question of coordination of activities; on this level, such coordination is actually impossible. It is, rather, a question of holding the organization together in the face of actual inconsistencies in its structure. It is thus highly probable that any pluralistic work organization will possess some integrative ideology, which may superficially assume the form of some organizational model or theory. Such ideological fictions may in fact be readily observed in many pluralistic work organizations as folk theories and strategies,[5] and have not infrequently caused sociological organization theory no end of trouble.

"Executive" departments. It is conceivable that integration could occur in the foregoing manner if only departments oriented to sectors were also oriented to relationships with other departments as such. It seems more likely that one or more specialized integrating departments will be found in typical pluralistic work organizations. These integrating departments will not be oriented to sectors at all, but rather to the mediation of relationships among departments that are. In "classical" bureaucracies, it would not be inaccurate to call such departments "executive" departments, inasmuch as they are particularly likely to appear at the top of the hierarchy, with the specifically sector-oriented departments at or near the bottom. However, in certain newly emerging forms of pluralistic organization, the integrative structure is itself apt to be pluralistic, and by

---

[5] See Robert D. Rossel, "The Ideology of Administration," unpublished doctoral dissertation, Yale University, 1967, for a comparative study of such ideological fictions in nine business and industrial organizations.

no means confined to the executive level.[6] We shall presently examine some of these forms. Meanwhile, it is not inaccurate to say that modern industrial work organizations exist in a continuous state of flux, have persistent tendencies to fall apart, and hold themselves together only by reason of a combination of ideological fictions and pluralistic ignorance. Unlike Moses, modern management faces the problem of keeping not only the crowd, but themselves as well, away from the mountain.[7]

EMPIRICAL EVIDENCE

Our theoretical argument suggests two general hypotheses:

1. As work organizations become technologically determined, they become differentiated into four separate departments, oriented respectively to the production, social, and scientific sectors of the environment, and to the problem of integration.
2. Modern industrial firms, however additionally complex they may be, will be minimally differentiated into these four departments, as pluralistic work organizations.

Empirical evidence with which to confront these hypotheses is quite fragmentary. Its diversity combined with its consistency, however, perhaps makes it quite convincing despite its incompleteness. Our first set of data is drawn from the material we have used throughout the book, and shows relationships between contractual development and apparently incipient pluralism. The second set of data is drawn from a recent independent study by Lawrence and Lorsch of differentiation and its implications in a sample of modern industrial firms.

Contractual Work and Differentiation

Despite the fact that no organizations in our sample emerged as clearly pluralistic, many of them exhibited various patterns of internal differentiation. In most cases such differentiation could readily be ascribed to simple division of labor or to particular external circumstances reproduced in the organization through social determination. In a few instances, however, patterns of differentiation appear with boundaries corresponding to those predicted by our theory of pluralistic development. In some organizations, a specialized group of people was concerned with defining and evaluating production objectives, quite apart from other organization operations. Among these organizations were some in which specialization

---

[6] See Lawrence and Lorsch, *Organization and Environment,* pp. 44-49.
[7] Exodus XIX: 24.

was carried further, with a second differentiated group concerned with matters involving technology and physical production apart from socio-cultural concerns. A few of the latter cases, in turn, separated general technological roles—usually involving problems of planning and design—from specific production roles. It was thus possible to classify many of the work organizations in our sample according to degree of differentiation along pluralistic lines, as follows:

1. Undifferentiated organizations.
2. Organizations with specialized units dealing with production objectives.
3. Organizations with specialized units dealing with production objectives, and specialized units concerned with physical technology.
4. Organizations with specialized units dealing with production objectives, specialized units dealing with general technology, and specialized units dealing with physical production.

To be sure, this scheme does not exactly fit our model of pluralistic development, but it seems to resemble it quite closely. Definition and evaluation of production objectives is at least part of the social sector, "general technological roles" appear analogous to the scientific sector, the production sector emerges clearly as such, and a residuum is left that presumably could include integrative functions. The main problem is the status of the social sector. Theoretically it ought to include, for example, recruitment of personnel; but does not seem to in any of our cases. The general impression on this score is that the organizations involved here, though perhaps in a transitional state, are still essentially socially determined. Such matters as recruitment therefore do not emerge as objects of direct organizational concern. This impression is far from clear, however.

Despite these difficulties, let us assume that this classification does represent progressively greater differentiation along pluralistic lines. If we assume this, we discover that the results of a cross-tabulation of this classification with our earlier typology of contractual work arrangements is strikingly consistent with our first hypothesis, as Table 4.1 shows. It indeed appears to be the case that, as contractual organizations move closer to technological determination, they tend to become differentiated along pluralistic lines, as our theory would suggest.

The preceding tendency is true only of the contractual organizations in our sample. Production determined organizations often have specialized parts, but not particularly along these lines; for one thing, production objectives are already set, and are thus not "dealt with" by the organization either in whole or in part. Familial and political organizations—par-

Table 4.1

Stage of Contractual Organization and Differentiation

Extent of differentiation

Stage of contractual organization	None	Objectives vs. other	Objectives vs. technology and production vs. other	Objectives vs. general technology vs. production vs. other
Diffuse	9	19	0	0
Job-specific	0	13	2	0
Occupationally based	0	0	1	7

ticularly the latter—do occasionally exhibit specialized units dealing with production objectives, but they do not seem ever to pass beyond this point in developing pluralistic differentiation patterns. It would seem that contractual recruitment ultimately makes pluralistic differentiation possible, probably through technological determination and consequent adaptive responses to inconsistencies in the work system.

Modern Industrial Firms

Our model of pluralistic work organization suggests, too, that modern industrial firms would be differentiated in strikingly similar basic ways, and would therefore face similar kinds of integrative problems. A recent study by Lawrence and Lorsch [8] lends considerable support to this contention. To be sure, the purposes of the Lawrence and Lorsch study are not wholly coincident with our own. Lawrence and Lorsch are more concerned with differences between types of industrial firms and their subunits than with accounting for similarities. Nevertheless, many of their results bear directly on questions we have posed and are readily adaptable to our purposes. The author is very much indebted to their work, not only for providing some empirical support to his own, but also for assistance in clarifying and developing many of the ideas expressed here about pluralistic work organization generally.

The fundamental thesis of Lawrence and Lorsch is that since different organizations face different environmental demands, there is no "one best way" of structuring work organization generally. The most effective organizational form is, rather, contingent upon the nature of environmental demands. Hence, when effectiveness and efficiency are held con-

[8] Lawrence and Lorsch, *Organization and Environment, passim.*

stant, differences in environmental structure imply not only differences in organization structure, but also differences in the kinds of problems with which organizations are confronted, as well, possibly, as differences in the kinds of people best suited to cope with these problems.

The relevance of the Lawrence and Lorsch study to pluralism lies in the fact that they chose to focus on differentiation and integration, both of environment and organization, as central concepts. All pluralistic work organizations face more or less differentiated environmental demands; such demands affect the required degree and form of differentiation in the organization structure both within and between departments, and thus imply that some patterns of organization will be more conducive to effective performance than others. The Lawrence and Lorsch findings are readily adaptable to our purposes because their conception of "organization" corresponds to what we mean by "work organization," and their conception of "environment" corresponds, in our scheme, to all elements of the work system exclusive of the work organization itself; that is, social setting, production objectives, and technology. Their findings as to how "environments" are viewed by organizations as being differentiated into sectors, and how organizations are oriented to different sectors, and with what consequences, are therefore directly relevant to our model.

Sectors. Lawrence and Lorsch studied six plastics manufacturing companies, two companies manufacturing containers, and two consumer food concerns. Their choice of organizations was based on a desire to study environments reflecting different rates of technological change and differing market problems, as well as organizations with different performance characteristics. Two of their findings, of relatively minor import to them, are of major import to us. First, they found it realistic to analyze all 10 of these companies as oriented to three separate sectors in the work system, which they term the "scientific," "market," and "techno-economic" sectors, respectively. Their "scientific" sector corresponds precisely to ours of the same name, and their "techno-economic" to our "production" sector. The "market" sector in their study represents only part of our "social" sector, but probably the most important part from the point of view of modern business management.

As with us, this tripartite division does not merely represent a conceptual framework; it turns out to be a very concrete characteristic of work systems. Not only did boundaries between sectors represent boundaries between departments in all 10 organizations, but characteristics of departments in any given sector proved, in all cases (though in varying degrees and ways), to differ from characteristics of departments in other sectors.

Departments. Second, Lawrence and Lorsch found all 10 organizations themselves to be differentiated into departments, all of which were oriented to one sector only, and with more than one department involved in a single sector in some instances. Specifically, the plastics firms each had four functional departments (sales, production, applied research, and basic research); the container firms, three (research, production, and sales); and the consumer food companies, four (production, research, sales, and marketing).

Differentiation. Lawrence and Lorsch then proceed to their main interest—the development and explanation of differences through this scheme between the plastics, container, and food environments, and between high-performing and low-performing companies in each one. They find that sectors differ from one another according to clarity of information, uncertainty of causal relations, and length of time between performance and feedback. Differences between sectors obtain in all three environments, but the character of these differences varies from one environment to another. For example, from these dimensions Lawrence and Lorsch were able to construct an uncertainty score for each sector in each environment. All sectors in the plastics firms were more uncertain than any sector in the container companies. Furthermore, in the plastics firms, the science sector was the most uncertain and the techno-economic sector the least, whereas in the container firms the techno-economic sector was the most uncertain, and the market sector the least. The foods concerns exhibited the same ordering as did the plastics firms, but with a lower over-all degree of uncertainty.

Degree of uncertainty in sector was found, also, to be related to various structural characteristics of departments oriented to the sector concerned, when performance was held constant. For example, under conditions of high performance, high degrees of uncertainty were associated with less formality in organization and more interpersonal styles of management, as one might theoretically expect. The investigators' general conclusion on this score was that the attributes of functional departments in high-performing organizations had a better fit to the technical requirements of sector structure than was the case in low-performing organizations.

Integration. Lawrence and Lorsch also present findings with respect to integration and its relationship to differentiation that are relevant for our purposes. They uncovered a tendency in low-performing organizations toward insufficient integration relative to the degree of sector differentiation. Furthermore, the greater the differences between sectors, the greater the difficulty of integration among departments oriented to different sectors. Success in performance was found to depend upon a degree of integration commensurate with differentiation.

Lawrence and Lorsch also devote a good deal of attention to various ways of achieving integration. One interesting finding is that a relatively high degree of integration can be achieved merely without differentiating enough in the first place, but only at considerable cost to performance. Precisely, this is done by deemphasizing technical problems in differentiation, thus achieving integration on more social grounds. In our scheme, this procedure would be analogous to a partial return to socially determined work organization, and such a tendency seems to have been found in low-performing organizations.

For Lawrence and Lorsch a more important process for achieving integration is to confront the problem resulting in divisiveness directly, with the people concerned working out a solution to it. They find a high relative emphasis on this mode of resolution to be characteristic of high-performing organizations. At first thought this finding would appear to contradict our contention that problems of integration between sectors cannot be attacked by confronting actual operations directly. However, on closer examination it turns out that this finding by no means contradicts our contention. Lawrence and Lorsch find as well that in such a confrontation it is important that the problem be specifically and narrowly delimited, so that the conflict it involves does not perseverate. They also find it realistic to treat integration as primarily a problem of conflict resolution, rather than one of routine administrative planning. In addition, confrontation of the problem itself is always accompanied by other measures, such as "smoothing over" differences, and, occasionally, "forcing" acceptance of a decision by essentially political means. It thus appears that conflict resolution is to a very great degree defined as an interpersonal process rather than a purely technical one. Persons having certain characteristics, furthermore, were found generally to be more effective at it than others; the most important characteristic in this respect proved to be ascribed expertise.

As for the character of integrative devices themselves, Lawrence and Lorsch found that they may assume the form of an integrator in each functional department, who divides his time between performing his role in the sector in which he works, and dealing with other departments; or a certain number of full-time integrators; or, some combination of the two. Integrators may function as individuals or in groups, which are often formally established for the purpose of acting as integrators.

The over-all results of the Lawrence and Lorsch study thus lend general support to our model of pluralistic work organization. Such organizations were found to be divided into sectors and departments in the way predicted by our model, with integration a problem depending for its solution on a variety of interpersonal devices apart from actual operations, as our model likewise predicts. The Lawrence and Lorsch findings also suggest, as we have, an over-all pressure toward reversion to socially determined forms of work. In their findings, this pressure takes two forms: 1) the possibility of achieving integration through insufficient technical differentiation, and 2) the importance of interpersonal style in response to both uncertainty and the demands for conflict resolution.

CONCLUSION

Although we have been unable to test our model of the development of pluralistic organization directly, in the sense that we have not observed any pluralistic organization in the actual process of development, we have been able to show a relationship between pluralistic differentiation and technological determination, under contractual conditions. We have also been able to predict from our model certain basic characteristics of modern industrial firms, and show that such firms do in fact possess the predicted characteristics. Specifically, modern industrial firms are pluralistic in structure. They consist of differentiated departments oriented to three broad sectors, each of which represents a consistent set of relationships in the work system, and all of which, taken together, include all of the basic relationships in the work system. Furthermore, it appears that no one single department is in fact oriented to more than one sector. Departments, however, may be oriented to other departments as such, which, in turn, can be oriented to different sectors. Indeed, it is essential that such a pattern be present if adequate integration of the work organization is to be achieved.

Fundamental Sources of Strain

Integration vs. differentiation. There is thus a fundamental strain between integration and differentiation in the modern industrial firm, a strain that goes far deeper than the usual pressures involved in the simple coordination of a specialized division of labor. The different sectors to which the firm is oriented entail activities that, ultimately, are inherently inconsistent. Perfect integration is therefore never possible on the functional level. A sufficient degree of normative integration to result in persistence of the firm is, however, possible, since efforts at integration take place between departments, rather than sectors as such. But the latent functional problems remain.

Technological vs. social determination. There is a second fundamental source of strain in the modern industrial firm: the strain between technological and social determination, which we examined in Chapter Three. Technological determination, though suggested and stimulated by the exigencies of modern industrial technology, is never complete, and is itself socially supported by recruitment based on a generalized occupational structure. Furthermore, members of the work organization are recruited from society at large, and thus invariably bring to the organization a variety of external social characteristics that are very likely to be relevant to work, if only because, in the last analysis, they are essential to personal motivation. The fact that pluralistic organization permits, through its differentiation into sectors, the manifest inclusion of these social characteristics in the organization itself at some point, makes the strain between technological and social determination an internal organizational matter.

We thus conclude that the inconsistencies intrinsic to any work system are, in modern industrial work, felt internally in the work organization, and specifically assume the form of a dual opposition: integration versus differentiation, and technological determination versus social determination.

Because the questions of integration versus differentiation and technological versus social determination are, according to our argument, the two most fundamental dilemmas of modern industrial work organization, we would expect a very wide range of particular problems of industrial organization ultimately to be traceable to these two dilemmas. We need not enumerate and analyze in detail all of the problems confronting modern industry to discover whether or not this contention is realistic. Certain major approaches to the study of organized industrial work yield presumptive evidence, under the assumption that persistent, important problems will generate systematic ways of studying and dealing with them. Four of the most important of these approaches can be derived through a systematic variation of assumptions about the states of the two dialectical processes we have identified. Table 5.1 shows these principal approaches as they derive from these two problems.

Table 5.1

Models of Modern Industrial Work

	Integration	Differentiation
Technological determination	Classical	Decision making
Social determination	Human relations	Natural systems

CHAPTER FIVE

Some Problems of Modern Industrial Work

FOUR APPROACHES

All four of these approaches can be viewed as representing special, and to some extent ideal-typical, instances of the general case of pluralistic work organization. Each one succeeds in simplifying this general case by making certain assumptions about the resolution of the two dilemmas we have described. In doing so, each one necessarily neglects certain kinds of situations common to all pluralistic work organizations to which one or more of the other three approaches applies. None, therefore, presents a complete picture.

The Classical Model

The *classical model* assumes that the work organization is both perfectly integrated and entirely technologically determined. Production objectives, as well as the means for achieving them, are thus agreed upon by all participants, with no problems resulting from possible goal displacement. Furthermore, adequate motivation to participate is present and totally in accord with technological requirements. Such assumptions are very useful and powerful ones, and they permit a variety of inferences about the structure of such a work organization. As Weber first pointed out, any work organization is, under these assumptions, characterized broadly by highly specific jobs, systematic rules, a pyramid-shaped authority structure, impersonality, an emphasis on jobs as such rather than on people, and distribution of rewards according to position and performance.[1] Efficiency can in principle be maximized simply by rearranging jobs and altering rules until the combination that best reflects technological requirements is achieved, and administration is thereby freed from a potential morass of nepotism, traditional rules of thumb, and red tape, or worse.

The central message of this approach is that insofar as pluralistic work organizations are technically efficient, they will be so by virtue of possessing these characteristics; that to the extent that they do possess these features they will be very efficient indeed; and that considering the alternative ways of doing things found in human experience, the modern work organization structured along these lines is a very remarkable social invention. The classical model served historically as the main point of departure for organization research; it has been echoed in its essentials

[1] Max Weber, *Wirtschaft und Gesellschaft* (Tübingen: J. C. B. Mohr, 1947), pp. 650-78. For a general discussion of "classical" organization theory, see James G. March and Herbert A. Simon, *Organizations* (New York: John Wiley & Sons, Inc., 1958), pp. 12-33. So far as I am aware, we are indebted to March and Simon for the term "classical" applied in this context.

in a variety of quarters, including the American "scientific management" movement and the earlier "traditional" school of public administration.[2]

The Natural Systems Model

The *natural systems model* is literally the direct opposite of the classical model. It views the work organization not as an integrated system, but as a collection of differentiated groups. Furthermore, the main characteristics of these groups do not stem from a technological determination of the roles played by their members, but rather from the fact that their members possess a variety of goals, attitudes, and other characteristics, which become reinforced and patterned as a result of social interaction among members. As a result, some over-all pattern of organization structure and work performance emerges, with the various groups involved functioning as "building blocks." Since the organization is not viewed as technologically determined, the focus is not on efficiency but on motivation, variations in which are brought about by changes in group composition and membership characteristics. This emphasis is often accompanied by the entirely correct observation that no matter how technologically efficient a role system may be, the work will simply not be done unless the people involved are sufficiently motivated to do it. Implicit in this view, too, is the assumption that if such motivation is present, the state of integration of the organization will not matter.[3]

The Decision-making and Human Relations Models

Both the *decision-making* and the *human relations* model represent, in a way, middle courses between the classical and the natural systems model. The decision-making model assumes the work organization to be technologically determined, yet differentiated into parts. Action results from patterns of communication and information flow between differentiated units, which, on the basis of data available to them, make optimal decisions in a rational manner. The decisions are optimal, in principle, and made rationally, because all decision rules are assumed to be technologically determined. Problems of extraneous social motivations and goals thus do not arise.[4]

The human relations model represents a different kind of middle

---

[2] March and Simon, *Organizations,* pp. 12-33; L. H. Gulick and L. Urwick, eds., *Papers on the Science of Administration* (New York: Institute of Public Administration, 1937).

[3] See Alvin W. Gouldner, "Organizational Analysis," in *Sociology Today,* ed. Robert K. Merton *et al.* (New York: Basic Books, Inc., 1959), pp. 405-7.

[4] See March and Simon, *Organizations,* esp. pp. 136-212; Richard M. Cyert and James G. March, *A Behavioral Theory of the Firm* (Englewood Cliffs, N.J.: Prentice-Hall, Inc., 1963).

course. Like the natural systems model, it emphasizes social determination, but like the classical model, it assumes an integrated work organization. Specific patterns of motivation and activity therefore emerge from group interaction and member characteristics, but these present no problems for an organization assumed to be perfectly integrated, with objectives already decided upon. As with the classical model, the assumption of integration makes the human relations model a very powerful one as well. Since the organization is assumed to be integrated, the distribution of effort can be centrally controlled by manipulating the social characteristics entering the organization structure, and the interaction patterns among the work force. The organization is not assumed to be technologically determined, so such manipulation of effort suffices for adequate performance.[5]

It is very simple to criticize any one of these four models, merely by pointing to its failure to make assumptions opposite to the ones it does make. For example, the classical model, by not taking pressures toward differentiation and social determination into account, fails to consider the human and social factors in the work situation, or the possibility that making decisions about objectives and procedures may be a problem, or the further possibility that the contents of these two omitted areas may be involved in mutual interplay. The natural systems model similarly fails to consider that work, if it is to be accomplished, must be patterned in accordance with the requirements of some technology, or that what emerges from pluralistic group interaction may be something less than an integrated work organization, and may indeed not be an organization at all. The decision-making model does not take into account the possibility that socially derived motivations may enter into the decisional process, or that the degree of integration essential to the promulgation of uniform decision rules of concerted action may not result from differentiated units playing formal games with each other. And finally, the human relations model neglects the possibilities that the technological requirements of the work may set limits on motivation and group structure, and that, because of differentiation, the interests of all parties to the work organization may not be identical.

In a very real sense, however, such criticisms are unfair. Except, perhaps, for some extreme cases, no proponent of any of these approaches claims to be describing all aspects of organizational operations. Rather,

[5] The literature on this model is virtually endless. For this author, the spirit of this approach is captured nowhere better than in James C. Worthy, "Organization Structure and Employee Morale," *American Sociological Review*, 15 (1950), 169-79; and in Douglas MacGregor, *The Human Side of Enterprise* (New York: McGraw-Hill Book Company, 1960).

it appears that each of these approaches, aside from the classical model, arose as a result of an awareness of certain previously unrecognized problems in pluralistic organization, was designed expressly to deal with those particular problems, and in fact often does so quite effectively. What is significant for our purposes is that the existence and form of these four approaches is rather precisely predictable. The fact that the specific problems with which each one deals should be considered important, as well as the fact that no one of these approaches suffices to explain organizational behavior as a whole, follows from a general model of the nature of organized work.

MANAGERIAL STRATEGIES

We are still left with the question of how pluralistic work organizations in modern industry function as total entities. A clue to answering this question, at least in a general way, is provided by our initial conception of the work system as intrinsically unstable, combined with the fact that each of the four models we have described emerges not only as a basis of organizational theory and research, but also can assume the form of an applied managerial strategy. Actually, our model more properly predicts the appearance of these approaches as managerial strategies, rather than as analytical devices used by social scientists. In a very real sense these four approaches are predictable folk models, and the fact that they also double as scientific constructs could be greeted with as much horror by students of organization as interest on the part of students of ethnoscience. Furthermore, failure explicitly to recognize the dual character of these four approaches has at times led to considerable confusion. For example, the classical model has not infrequently been portrayed as a managerial strategy and then castigated as such, on the grounds that it does not provide an adequate organization theory. As we shall see presently, whether or not a model provides an adequate organization theory may be quite unrelated to the question of whether or not it can be an effective ideological basis of a managerial strategy.

Management as such takes on unprecedented importance in modern industrial work organizations, not only because such organizations are ordinarily very large, but also because of the severe integrative problems they present. Modern management must cope with a functionally inconsistent system of activities, whose inconsistencies, in pluralistic organizations, appear largely as internal problems of organization structure. It must do so by successfully promoting sufficient normative integration to keep the system operating in the face of tendencies toward functional self-destruction. One would therefore expect to find, among successful managers, rather firm commitment to ideologically based managerial strategies.[6] Each of the four models we have discussed, furthermore, fulfills rather well the requirements of a successful ideology, and is hence suited to serve as the basis of a managerial strategy. Each one reflects reality to a sufficient degree to be credible, but at the same time neglects other potentially troublesome features of work organization. Each model is logically consistent internally and implies a rather definite course of action required to put its prescriptions into effect.[7]

In principle any one of these four models can serve as the basis of a more or less well-articulated managerial strategy, but theoretically we would expect the classical model to emerge most frequently in this form, because it is vigorous in assuming that the most knotty problems of pluralistic work organization—integration and technological determination—are either solved, or readily capable of solution. If the members of a pluralistic work organization firmly believe that both integration and technological determination are possible and desirable, they will tend to define problems in these areas as temporary aberrations, and a cultural basis will exist for continued effort despite the presence of actually insurmountable difficulties.

Judging by the polemical orientation of the applied literature generally, the classical strategy has been and probably still is the most prevalent basic strategy in organized industrial work, despite growing inroads of various "modern management" practices. Engineering treatises abound in prescriptions for strengthening the classical strategy, whereas more behaviorally oriented works usually begin by attacking it as a prevailing form and then prescribing a human relations strategy as a means of solving the problems that the classical strategy involves. Since the late 1930's, and partly in response to these prescriptions, instances have been increasing of the actual use of a human relations strategy, particularly in certain parts of work organizations. Recently a similar literature has begun to develop pointing out some of the difficulties which this strategy too entails, and advocating some other strategy as an appropriate response to these difficulties.

More recently, with the advent of computer technology and the growing feasibility of applying it to the solution of decisional problems in a differentiated pluralistic organization, some steps have likewise been taken in the direction of a decision-making, rather than a classical or a human

---

[6] See Francis X. Sutton et al., The American Business Creed (Cambridge, Mass.: Harvard University Press, 1956), pp. 53-66, 90-107; Reinhard Bendix, Work and Authority in Industry (New York: John Wiley & Sons, Inc., 1956); Wilbert E. Moore, The Conduct of the Corporation (New York: Random House, Inc., 1962), pp. 1-18.

[7] Sutton et al., The American Business Creed, pp. 1-15.

relations, strategy. These efforts are reflected in such procedures as management gaming and some forms of "project management," and are just beginning to emerge from the theoretical stage into actual application. The applied literature on work has paid very little attention to the problems that management systems based on a decision-making strategy would entail, coupled with the advocacy of some other strategy as a solution to these problems; the field of higher education does provide some examples of such criticisms, as does the field of politics, though many of these criticisms seem to occur on the streets rather than in the literature. As for manifest natural systems strategies, they are rather rare in work organization, inasmuch as natural systems ideology is not responsive to problems of integration and technology, but rather represents concessions on both of these fronts.

But such strategies are not absent from other kinds of organizations. Perhaps the best articulated natural systems strategy is the idealized "collegial" model popular in university circles. There is some reason to believe that this model serves the same function in higher education as does the classical model in work management practice. Some evidence exists that efforts at integration combined with technological determination inhibit productivity and innovation where multiple research projects are actually largely independent of one another in a common general organizational context.[8] A natural systems ideology is thus not uncommon in the university, and occasionally elements of it spill over into the scientific sector of pluralistic work organization.

Despite the fact that the classical strategy remains, as we would expect, the predominant one in pluralistic work organization, degree of conformity to this strategy is unlikely to be the same in all sectors of organizational operations, as the findings of Lawrence and Lorsch and others have indicated.[9] Advocacy of the classical strategy will typically be much stronger and will be met with more consensus in departments oriented to the production sector, together, probably, with departments concerned with over-all integration, than it will be in departments oriented to such activities as marketing and sales, and research and development. In marketing and sales, where integration combined with social relationships bulks large as a major problem, one is apt to find more stress on human relations ideology; in research and development, partic-

[8] Louis B. Barnes, *Organizational Systems and Engineering Groups* (Boston: Division of Research, Graduate School of Business Administration, Harvard University, 1960); Simon Marcson, *The Scientist in American Industry* (New York: Harper & Row, Publishers, 1960.

[9] Paul R. Lawrence and Jay W. Lorsch, *Organization and Environment* (Boston: Division of Research, Graduate School of Business Administration, Harvard University, 1967), pp. 44-49.

ularly if either the company or the department members are interested in anything approaching pure research, one discovers elements of natural systems strategy.[10] Nevertheless, the assumption that the classical strategy will predominate in pluralistic organized work probably remains realistic.

TENSIONS AND PROBLEMS IN
PLURALISTIC WORK ORGANIZATION

We may now describe the way in which the inconsistencies intrinsic to work systems generally emerge in modern industrial work. We have identified four basic administrative strategies, each of which is based on the assumption of some ideal combination of possibilities contained in the two dichotomies of integration versus differentiation, and technological determination versus social determination. Our discussion of these administrative strategies suggests that the application of any one of them generates problems. These problems stem from the fact that the organization also possesses characteristics opposite to those that the strategy assumes to be the "natural state" of affairs. Thus the application of a classical strategy leads to problems arising from the fact that the organization is also a natural system. The reverse of this statement is likewise true, but not especially relevant for our purposes, since natural systems strategies as such seldom appear in organized work, and when they do, are decidedly not dominant. Similarly, the application of a human relations strategy evokes difficulties because the organization is at the same time a decision-making system. Both this statement, and its reverse, that application of a formal decisional strategy generates human relations problems, are relevant to our concern: as we shall see presently, both human relations and decision-making strategies—particularly the former—are likely to appear at least as important subordinate strategies in pluralistic work organization.

The principal consequence of the appearance, as problems, of organizational characteristics opposite to those assumed by the strategy being followed necessarily evokes some effort to deal with those problems. At the very least, the people motivated by these opposite characteristics will behave in accordance with them—and hence in a sense deal with the problem themselves—whether or not top administrators take any official action. In the case of no action on the part of top administrators, we would predict that a classically managed pluralistic work organization will turn into a natural system and disintegrate. But since any observable work organization is perforce still there, we conclude that this has not

[10] Lawrence and Lorsch, *Organization and Environment*, pp. 44-49.

happened in any of them, and thus infer that management has adopted some deviation from a classical strategy to cope with the situation.

Two courses of action are open. One is to concede integration while maintaining technological determination, and thereby shift to a decision-making strategy. The other is to concede technological determination while maintaining integration, and thus change to a human relations approach. It is of course not necessary that such shifts occur in a uniform way throughout the entire organization. Strategies can differ in both kind as well as degree of consistency from one department to another, and indeed, as we have seen, differences in sector structure suggest that they are very likely so to differ, and along broadly predictable lines. Of these two possible shifts, the one more likely to occur has been the shift to a human relations strategy. The reason for this does not stem from any inherent advantages of human relations over decisional strategies, but rather from the fact that until very recently the kinds of knowledge and hardware necessary to devise and implement technologically determined decisional routines appropriate to highly differentiated organizational situations have not existed. They still must be said to be in their infancy, despite impressive recent developments.

The bulk of the literature in the management field, therefore, as well as in organization theory deriving largely from the study of work, is concerned with relationships between classical and human relations strategies, stemming from the conflict between the classical and natural systems models. Since several excellent reviews of this literature appear elsewhere, we shall not attempt a comprehensive review here.[11] It is however noteworthy that most of this literature is devoted to problems arising from integrative administrative practices in the classical strategy, rather than to problems arising from technological determination. The administrative difficulties are viewed as the ones to be solved. Hence integration is to remain, and the theme expounded is that integration can remain if social factors are taken into account in organization; that is, if a shift occurs away from technological determination, which is implicitly viewed as dispensable, or at least less important than integration. This position leads to a human relations strategy. Thus MacGregor's classic contrast of "Theory X" versus "Theory Y" is concerned mainly with problems of supervisory style and the ways in which authority is exercised generally in the classical approach, pointing out that the classical strategy encourages dependency relationships and reduces self-motivation through the repression of self-expression.[12] According to Mac-Gregor, a shift to a human relations strategy, with more participation in

11 See especially Peter M. Blau and W. Richard Scott, *Formal Organizations* (San Francisco: Chandler Publishing Company, 1962), pp. 258-301.
12 MacGregor, *The Human Side of Enterprise*, pp. 33-43.

management by workers, will among other things go far toward obviating such problems, and do so in a way entirely consistent with maintaining integration. In fact, MacGregor explicitly characterizes "Theory Y"—the human relations strategy—as embodying "the *integration* of individual and organizational goals," [13] an integration which, in conformance with the human relations model, he holds to be both possible and desirable. Similarly, the "new patterns of management" that Likert proposes are designed mainly to deal with problems of supervisory style at the work group level.[14]

One of the most comprehensive models of the way in which classical administrative strategies generate problems as a result of failure to take account of natural systems elements is set forth by Argyris. In his various works, he characterizes the classical strategy as entailing a variety of administrative assumptions and practices, prolonged exposure to which tends to result in the generation of actually pathological personal conditions. These not only may be damaging to mental health on the individual level, but also inhibit the capacities of people to behave in innovative and productive ways as organization members.[15] The significant fact about Argyris' work is that he does not present a simple human relations solution to these problems. The path toward their resolution ultimately lies in the design of new organizational strategies, which permit the expressive elements inherent in natural systems to emerge, yet at the same time recognize that the organization is simultaneously a pattern of parts and an integrated whole.[16] For Argyris, the search is still on, and the result to be hoped for is a new strategy quite different from any of the four that we have described as the most likely ones to develop "naturally."

A second, less frequently encountered version of the problems of the classical strategy focuses on difficulties arising from technological determination, rather than on administrative problems per se. Workers continually exposed to certain purely technological demands tend to develop various personal reactions, stemming from the fact that the organization is also a natural system. Prolonged exposure to assembly line work, for example, has been found to lead to job dissatisfaction, high turnover and absentee rates, as well as generalized social apathy.[17] The extent and kind

[13] *Ibid.,* p. 45.

[14] Rensis Likert, *New Patterns of Management* (New York: McGraw-Hill Book Company, 1961).

[15] See especially Chris Argyris, *Integrating the Individual and the Organization* (New York: John Wiley & Sons, Inc., 1964).

[16] *Ibid.,* pp. 148-54.

[17] Charles R. Walker and Robert H. Guest, *The Man on the Assembly Line* (Cambridge, Mass.: Harvard University Press, 1952), esp. pp. 115-22; Ely Chinoy, *Automobile Workers and the American Dream* (Garden City, N.Y.: Doubleday & Company, Inc., 1955).

of such reactions is, furthermore, a function of the kind of technology involved.[18] Job lot production, for instance, entails fewer problems of this variety than does assembly line work. Continuous flow production, with automation, obviates some of the social difficulties of assembly line work, but generates further problems of its own, stemming from the rather intense concentration that tending such processes often demands.[19]

This literature is less extensive than the literature focussing on supervisory and administrative styles. Perhaps the reason is that its formal properties make it difficult for it to lead to very many concrete proposals for solving the problems it uncovers in a human relations context. Unlike the human relations literature on supervisory style, it assumes implicitly and, we might add, entirely realistically, that some technological determination will remain as a continuing feature of modern industrial work. This assumption makes it difficult to propose solutions that strictly follow the human relations "line," except in the form of relaxation of technological requirements, or changing the technology itself to allow room for more social expression. This type of proposal is illustrated by such measures as job enlargement, bank building, alteration of patterns and speeds of assembly lines, and so forth.[20]

Since this body of research assumes a continuing technological orientation, it actually lends itself better to solutions via differentiation than to solutions via social determination. Moreover, as formal decisional strategies have become increasingly realistic possibilities, this research has tended to take the former direction despite its initial place in the human relations tradition. Thompson, for example, in a recent work, starts with technological demands, and then indicates a resolution to the problems they generate in the direction of a decision-making model, which reduces conflict as a result of explicit recognition of differentiation, explicitly eschewing human relations strategies designed to reduce conflict by introducing social elements.[21] Thompson explicitly characterizes "complex purposive organizations" as "natural systems subject to rationality

[18] Robert Blauner, *Alienation and Freedom* (Chicago: University of Chicago Press, 1964).

[19] Blauner, *Alienation and Freedom;* also see Charles Perrow, "A Framework for the Comparative Analysis of Organizations," *American Sociological Review,* 32 (1967), 194-208; Charles R. Walker, *Toward the Automatic Factory* (New Haven: Yale University Press, 1957).

[20] Walker and Guest, *The Man on the Assembly Line,* pp. 115-22; Charles R. Walker, "The Problem of the Repetitive Job," *Harvard Business Review,* 28 (1950), 54-58; Robert H. Guest, "Job Enlargement: A Revolution in Job Design," *Personnel Administration,* 20 (1957), 13-15.

[21] James D. Thompson, *Organizations in Action* (New York: McGraw-Hill Book Company, 1967).

norms." [22] In our terms, this suggests a decision-making strategy under conditions of differentiation, and Thompson sets forth a·number of propositions characterizing the operation of organizations under such a strategy.

Given a shift to either a human relations or a decision-making strategy, the tendencies we have described presumably do not stop, but continue to produce further shifts, each in turn generating its own tendencies for a change to another form in the way we have described. The literature is sparse on the kinds of shifts engendered by a decision-making strategy, and in defense of this situation it must be said that such a strategy is as yet rare on a very large scale in modern industrial work. Our model would predict a tendency for such a strategy to evoke counterstrategies of either a classical or a natural systems nature. Thompson gives some indication that this opposition may occur, by noting that highly differentiated decisional situations may be met either by a reversion to classical strategy through the imposition of centralized power or by a movement toward a natural system through coalition formation and political maneuvering.[23] A similar finding is reported in a recent study by Baldridge, which, however, deals with a university, and not a work organization as we have defined that concept.[24]

The literature is a bit more copious on problems evoked by human relations strategies, though here again, exploration of relevant mechanisms is far from complete. Our model would predict either a movement in the direction of a natural systems strategy (which, if complete and widespread in a work organization, would probably result in its dissolution), or a reversion to a classical strategy. Most of the social criticisms of human relations practices stress the very real possibility that, in the last analysis, the workers may forcibly discover that management was following a classical strategy after all, with technological determination. If, for example, classical strategy dictates that a number of workers should be laid off, the workers are very apt to find themselves without jobs, despite the fact that the layoff may have been fully communicated in accord with the best human relations tenets, including giving the workers an opportunity to discuss it.[25] More formal studies, too, indicate that human relations measures may boggle in the face of ultimately technologically determined exigencies. Participatory management, for example, has not always been found to be very efficient, and managers who have

[22] *Ibid.*, p. 144.
[23] *Ibid.*, pp. 132-43.
[24] J. Victor Baldridge, "Power and Conflict in the University," unpublished doctoral dissertation, Yale University, 1968.
[25] Amitai Etzioni, *Modern Organizations* (Englewood Cliffs, N.J.: Prentice-Hall, Inc., 1964), pp. 43-44.

been through sensitivity training programs have not always found it easy to behave as they were trained when they return to their regular jobs.[26]

It would appear, on the basis of this rather cursory review of the literature, not only for its findings but also for the reflection it offers of problems faced in modern management practice, that inconsistencies intrinsic to work systems are felt in the modern industrial firm as well. There they take the form of opposing managerial strategies, none of which is entirely satisfactory, and each of which sets forces in motion that tend to produce a shift to another strategy. The modern industrial firm retains its cultural definition as a unitary entity in the face of functional conflict by settling upon a dominant administrative strategy as an ideology, and constantly shifting this ideology in response to visible exigencies. In appearance it thus resembles a kaleidoscope, with different parts operating according to different strategies, and with shifts constantly occurring in strategy in each part, according to the tendencies we have outlined.

The most frequent current pattern appears to be a dialectic between classical and human relations strategies, though with the advent of computer technology, decision-making strategies appear likely to enter the picture with increasing frequency. The success of the enterprise seems to depend upon constant change, wherein no one strategy is pursued constantly or consistently enough to render its shortcomings visible, or at least to result in their becoming defined as irreparable. Integration, differentiation, technological determination, and social determination are all, like prosperity, "just around the corner," and the corner is kept in sight but never rounded.

CONCLUSION

Our tour of organized work has started with the most primitive conditions and has ended with modern industry. But in one sense we have never left home. Organized work exists everywhere, at all times and in all places. In its most basic respects, work is everywhere the same. It entails the imposition of social forms of organization on a structure of physical exigencies. This juxtaposition of the social and physical can take various forms, some of which depend on the state of social and technological development, and some of which are matters of choice. All of them, however, involve the intrinsic difficulty that social organization can never fully satisfy technological demands, and that technological characteristics can never fully reflect social reality.

Organized work therefore always represents a compromise between

[26] Blau and Scott, *Formal Organizations,* pp. 124-28.

physical and social forces. Like any compromise, organized work is never achieved without costs. Extremely primitive settings typically demand a rather high degree of efficiency in work. Organized work in primitive societies by and large delivers such efficiency, but only at the price of being intermittent, relatively noninnovative, and not well integrated with social structure. In contrast, the institutions of more traditional societies make for close linkages between work organization and social structure, but only at a cost of considerable inefficiency and a progressive maladaptation to industrial conditions.

This situation, as we have seen, poses acute problems in modernization insofar as organized work is concerned, problems that can be overcome only in the presence of certain external conditions and their interplay with the structure of work organization. The route toward modernization, insofar as organized work is concerned, takes the form of a progressive narrowing of social influences on work through various kinds of contractual arrangements, combined with a growing technological orientation on the part of work organizations. Pluralistic work organization is the eventual result.

Pluralistic work itself is similarly a compromise between physical and social forces. It too involves costs. To be sure, pluralistic work can be permanently sustained, innovative, relatively efficient, and reasonably well integrated with social structure. It is, likewise, well adapted to industrial conditions. Its costs do not lie in these areas, and in this sense it is quite different from preindustrial work forms. Rather, the costs of pluralistic work organization are a highly technologically based social structure, combined with integrative problems within the work organization of unprecedented proportions. Efforts to cope with these costs are reflected in a variety of shifting managerial strategies.

In sum, perhaps the most striking single feature of organized work is that it occurs at all. Organized work is everywhere a major ongoing activity. Nevertheless it is always unstable and borders on the impossible. That "man's work is never done" is no mere proverb. It is perhaps our fate to be continuously driven to achieve what never can be accomplished.

This appendix provides some supplementary methodological discussion of the cross-cultural study appearing in Chapter Two.

GENERAL REMARKS

Although this author has used the cross-cultural method with large numbers of societies quite frequently in his previous work, this method is not, on the whole, used very much; at times it has been the subject of some controversy. Briefly, cross-cultural analysis is the comparative study of social phenomena over a sample of several societies. It is particularly useful when one's research design requires the introduction of wide variations in the setting of whatever one is studying, and if the object of study can be meaningfully pursued in a pre-industrial context.

The general nature of this approach and the problems it entails have been discussed elsewhere by various people, including the author. No effort will be made to summarize this literature here; the reader is directed to it for further information.[1] Suffice it to say that the study presented in Chapter Two by and large exhibits no more and no fewer difficulties than do our previous cross-cultural studies of work. The one possible exception to this claim lies in the

[1] See in particular Frank W. Moore, ed., *Readings in Cross-Cultural Methodology* (New Haven: HRAF Press, 1961); Stanley H. Udy, Jr., "Cross-Cultural Analysis: A Case Study," in *Sociologists at Work,* ed. Phillip E. Hammond (New York: Basic Books, Inc., 1964), pp. 161-83.

APPENDIX

"scale" of social development we employ. The possible problem does not lie in the inductive use of scale analysis of cross-sectional data to infer a developmental sequence. As explained in the text, that is not what we have done, though the result may superficially resemble such an effort. Rather, we have constructed a typology that makes no claims about sequences of traits, and we have done this from a deductive line of reasoning based on necessary but not sufficient conditions.[2] However, the cross-sectional nature of our sample still remains, and as a result we cannot differentiate societies "prone to development" (for whatever reason) from those societies not prone to development. Possible interaction effects of "proneness to development" relative to the relationships between social structure and work organization are hence uncontrolled, and it is at least conceivable that they could in fact be such as to render our present results misleading. We have no way of assessing whether or not this has happened.

CODING

With the exceptions indicated below, all coding was done by the author and an assistant. The results of an initial independent coding were compared, discrepancies were discussed, and an effort made to reach a consensus in cases of disagreement. Initial agreement emerged about 75 percent to 80 percent of the time for any given variable, with eventual agreement reached through discussion on an additional 10 percent to 15 percent of the cases. Cases on which agreement could not be reached were not used in those parts of the analysis involving the codes about which disagreement existed.

There were three exceptions to this procedure. First, in categorizing the sample of societies, Murdock's codes for sedentary agriculture, centralized government, and complex stratification were used.[3] Second, for the various characteristics of authority structure and functional complexity, codes from a previous study by the author were used.[4] Third, in categorizing work organizations, cases where partial agreement was reached were retained in the analysis by the procedures described on pp. 34-35.

---

[2] Above, pp. 24-27.

[3] George P. Murdock, "World Ethnographic Sample," *American Anthropologist,* 59 (1957), 664-87.

[4] Stanley H. Udy, Jr., *Organization of Work* (New Haven: HRAF Press, 1959).

SAMPLING

It is not possible for any cross-cultural study using secondary materials to employ a clearly unbiased sample of societies, if only because one's population is limited to societies that have been studied. One is further limited to those societies offering adequate materials. It is necessary, therefore, consciously to select societies on this basis, while at the same time avoiding clustering in some particular culture area. Furthermore, in studies such as ours, which are partly exploratory, it is desirable to use as many societies as possible so as to permit maximum "exploration."

Our sampling procedure was thus designed to take these conditions into account insofar as possible. First, from each of the 60 world sub-regions designated in Murdock's "World Ethnographic Sample," up to four societies known to offer particularly adequate materials on organized work were selected.[5] This procedure left only seven subregions unrepresented. Societies were then chosen randomly in each of these seven sub-regions until one society offering at least some usable data on work organization was found in each subregion.[6] Despite our efforts, "North and Central India" remained unrepresented.

The over-all result of this procedure was a sample of 125 societies distributed as follows over the six major world culture areas designated by Murdock:

1. Africa	23
2. Circum-Mediterranean	15
3. East Eurasia	19
4. Insular Pacific	22
5. North America	26
6. South America	20
Total	125

The societies in the sample are shown below, classified according to developmental type (see above, pp. 30-31).

Type I

Aleut	Copper Eskimo	Paiute
Andamanese	Murngin	Sinkaietk
Aranda	Nambicuara	Tubatulabal
Blackfoot	Naron	Wintun

[5] *American Anthropologist*, 59, 664-87.
[6] "Overseas Europe" and "Northwest Europe" were combined in this process.

Type II

Caingang	Kwakiutl	Samoyed
Chukchee	Lapps	Siriono
Gilyak	Ojibwa	Timbira
Haida	Ona	Yokuts

Type IIII

Apalai	Ifugao	Tarahumara
Atayal	Ila	Tenetehara
Buka	Iroquois	Terena
Cagaba	Jivaro	Tikopia
Camayura	Kabyles	Trumai
Carib	Karen	Tupinamba
Cayapa	Kikuyu	Turkana
Dard	Kiwai	Winnebago
Dogon	Lobi	Wogeo
Fang,	Navaho	Yagua
Havasupai	Papago	Yami
Hopi	Pukapukans	Yaqui
Iban	Tallensi	Zulu
Ifaluk	Taos	Zuni

Type IV

Aymara	Jukun	Nuer
Azande	Kazak	Osset
Bedouin	Malekulans	Penobscot
Bemba	Mangaians	Samoans
Betsileo	Maori	Somali
Chagga	Maricopa	Sotho
Crow	Marshallese	Tahitians
Cuna	Mbundu	Tarasco
Fijians	Menomini	Tigre
Gond	Muong	Tiv
Hottentot	Mzab	Trobrianders
Hutsul		

Type V

Afghans	English	Nyoro
Ashanti	Germans	Romans
Babylonians	Haitians	Songhai
Belu	Hazara	Telugu
Burmese	Iranians	Thai
Burusho	Macassarese	Tibetans
Cambodians	Malay	Tuareg
Chinese	Mam	Wolof
Dahomeans		

SOURCE MATERIALS

We shall not attempt here to provide a bibliography of all sources consulted, for it would be quite extensive and would in large part repeat a bibliography we have already compiled and published elsewhere, on organized work in nonindustrial society. The reader is thus referred to this earlier bibliography for references.[7] For additional materials, he is referred to the Human Relations Area Files, which were used as much as possible in the cross-cultural analysis in Chapter Two.[8]

[7] Udy, *Organization of Work*, pp. 159-77.
[8] For descriptions and discussions of the Human Relations Area Files, see Moore, *Readings in Cross-Cultural Methodology;* also George P. Murdock *et al., Outline of Cultural Materials,* 4th ed. (New Haven: HRAF Press, 1961).